Mister Music Maker,
LAWRENCE WELK

by Mary Lewis Coakley

MISTER MUSIC MAKER, LAWRENCE WELK

———

OUR CHILD—GOD'S CHILD

FITTING GOD INTO THE PICTURE

Mister
Music Maker,
LAWRENCE WELK

MARY LEWIS COAKLEY

With a Foreword by Lawrence Welk

1958

DOUBLEDAY & COMPANY, INC.

Garden City, New York

Library of Congress Catalog Card Number 58–6634
Copyright © 1958 by Mary Lewis Coakley
All Rights Reserved
Printed in the United States of America

Foreword

It's a pleasant fact in life that, should a man be so blessed as to receive a more than ordinary measure of public acclaim, a lot of good people want to learn about his early struggles to achieve it. Several booklets and articles have been published on our accomplishments, and now the distinguished author, Mrs. Mary Lewis Coakley, has written this detailed and all-inclusive story of my life. Before doing so, Mrs. Coakley spent weeks at our home, getting to know my wife and family, then attended a good many of our musical rehearsals and professional engagements, becoming closely acquainted with my other family—the Champagne Music Makers. Her book, which follows, shows warm perception into what makes us tick and I am honored to be the subject of it. Our genuine thanks to Mrs. Coakley and to you, the public, whose gratifying interest in our work has justified her efforts.

Lawrence Welk

Contents

List of Illustrations

Mister Music Maker,
LAWRENCE WELK

Chapter 1

♫

"Strike Up the Band"

"Uh-one, and uh-two, and . . ." Lawrence Welk's hands
go up, his hands go down. He has popped a cork, and
Champagne Music fizzes gaily through the glittering ballroom of Washington's Mayflower Hotel.

A cameraman on the right of the bandstand maneuvers
his ungainly instrument. His helper swings the giant spotlight. Now swish gowns, and jewels almost as valuable as
an item in the national budget, come into focus.

Here is a night for Lawrence to cherish! It is January 21
of the year 1957, and this is an Inaugural Ball.

A penny for your thoughts, onetime farm boy, as you
stand up there on the stage and survey the room. You can
see the President in his box; you can see the diplomats,
the senators, the political party leaders, and other promi-
nent citizens—all swirling about to your bright tunes.

Actually Lawrence Welk will not speak his thoughts just
now, so I'll play at mind reading.

I'm watching his face. He flashes that trademark smile
of his, back and forth between his musicians and the milling people. Fifteen hundred watts bright tonight, it spells
out as clearly as a neon sign: I'M HAPPY. Even in the
very act of autographing programs for the crowd which

masses around the base of the bandstand, he fairly bounces up and down to the beat of the music, *allegro vivo*. When have I seen such tremendous relish in the living moment? And such joy of fulfillment? He must have dreamed about this night, and waited for it a long time.

Now a dancing couple jostles by me on the crowded floor, cutting off my view of Lawrence. "There have always been Inaugural Balls, since the beginning . . . This is the biggest thing in the country . . ." I overhear snatches of their conversation as they edge close to me, and my imagination veers to do a quick flash-back.

It shows Martha Washington herself sitting on a raised dais, while courtly eighteenth-century couples bow gracefully before her; it presents a close-up of Dolly Madison, elegant in velvet, as she tosses a provocative smile at the gentlemen, begging "the please of a dance, ma'am"; it pictures slim, spirited, "Princess Alice" Roosevelt, organizing a grand march which includes all her little brothers. Just before a fade-out, there's another scene—a glimpse of one of Lawrence's predecessors, Victor Herbert, playing for the McKinley Inauguration.

No doubt about it, this is, and has always been (of its kind), "the biggest thing in the country." I can understand why Lawrence has that exultant feeling. Could any bandleader ask for more than he has tonight?

But what's happening? I don't want to miss what's going on with my sentimentalizing and theorizing.

There's a stir, and necks are craning, but I can't make out what all the fuss is about. Now the crowd is parting a little. I crane my own neck. Why, I hadn't expected that! Somebody is escorting Lawrence Welk to the box of honor and there is the President extending his hand to clasp that of the bandleader.

Cameras are grinding away.

"That was a great moment!" Lawrence told me afterward in the gee-whiz tone of a little boy. "When I was back on the farm, I never thought I'd shake hands with a president of the United States."

"You've come a long way." I murmured the cliché, as I measured the full distance myself for the first time. This was indeed a far cry from the Dakota wheatlands. It was on those wide acres, stretching to the rim of a lonely world, that Lawrence was born and reared—and in a sod house which boasted no electricity, no phone, no plumbing, none of the conveniences labeled necessities by most Americans.

Would any seer or prophet have been bold enough to foretell that the road he took from the Dakotas would lead to an Inaugural Ball, and to the TV studios of Hollywood? If there had been even one, which is doubtful, he would scarcely have figured that Lawrence's gross earnings* in 1956 would hover around the three-million mark. There is a sum that most industrialists, or bank presidents—or for that matter the nation's President, who greeted Lawrence Welk at the Hotel Mayflower—can never hope to write on their income-tax reports.

For such success I can use Hollywood's pet word, colossal, and not even exaggerate. But how did Lawrence Welk attain such success? What is his secret?

Without formal education, without "knowing the right

* Before payroll and other extensive expenses.

people," without a background of money or prestige, he managed to pull off the stunt. How?

There is one rather obvious answer, and it is the right answer up to a point. Lawrence Welk won success largely the way other rugged Americans before him have done it, by working hard and seizing opportunity. He personifies the pristine American dream. His story is an American saga.

But, true as this is, it falls far short of the whole answer. The thing that makes Lawrence Welk special is not that he began his career with few material advantages and "made good." Other capable men before him have done that. It isn't that he has attained nationwide popularity through the highly competitive entertainment medium. Other gifted men have done that too. Rather, it is that he has won his bright laurels in the Hollywood arena without the support of the tried and tested props, without the gags, the gimmicks, or the glamour of the slick performers, the blasé wisecrackers, the glib comedians, and the publicity boys. To most of them he appears as a rustic personality who plays "corny" music.

Yet that personality must have some winning secret, and that music some charms which fascinate as surely as did the Pied Piper's melodies.

Whatever Lawrence Welk and his music have today he and his music have always had. His friends and fans insist: "Lawrence hasn't changed. He's just the same now as when I first knew him and the band back in Yankton, South Dakota . . . back in Pittsburgh . . . back at the Trianon in Chicago . . ."

The Hollywood experts are still baffled. Lawrence Welk is an inexplicable wonder in their gaudy and giddy world.

Indeed, he is almost unbelievable. After all this time they keep asking: "What's he got? How did he of all people get to the top of the heap? What makes the guy tick?"

I think I know the answers, and I hope that I can make them clear, though it may take a whole book to do it.

♫

Chapter 2

"On with the Show"

Writing about Lawrence Welk's career is rather like writing a mystery story or a mystery stage play. I saw him bestriding the heights of the entertainment world and then I had to undertake the long search backward through time and space—from 1958 to 1903, from Hollywood to the Dakotas, looking for clues to his success. Only by this procedure could I unravel knotty circumstance and find out precisely how he "arrived."

Also writing of the very man himself, his character and personality, had about it an element of mystery—in fact the more intriguing mystery. At first glance Lawrence Welk seemed to fit neatly, with no loose ends dangling, into the pigeonhole marked Naïve Country Boy. But as time went on, and I grew to know him better, and as I talked to numbers of his friends and confreres, I kept discovering new quirks in his personality, and these I could not so easily slip into a rigid category. Lawrence Welk, ingenuous though he is, is a much more complex being than I had had the gumption to realize from the start. It struck me that writing of Lawrence Welk, the man, is rather like working a jigsaw puzzle: I would find how one piece fitted with another and then with another until finally all the pieces fitted together, to form a whole rounded picture from which the man emerged.

The process began in the summer of 1956, six months before the Inauguration, and I intend to give a blow-by-blow account, taken from my notebook jottings. As the King directed *Alice in Wonderland's* white rabbit, I'll "begin at the beginning, go on till . . . the end, and then stop."

My transcontinental plane has landed. Here I am in Los Angeles, all set to beard the lion in his den—or Lawrence Welk in his home. I have been invited to stay there. I start walking toward the airport terminal, and I see a man doffing his hat to me. Ed Spaulding, Lawrence Welk's personal friend and confidant,* introduces himself, and makes a little welcoming speech: "The Welks are so happy to have you. If it's all right, we'll drive by the house to drop your bags, then we'll go on to the studio. Lawrence wants you there before the show goes on."

I like the man's gentle mannerliness. There is an old-fashioned courtesy about it. But I'm impressed with something else, too: this plan is precision-timed by Lawrence Welk, so to dillydally is clearly out of order.

Could be that "Uh-one, and uh-two, and . . ." is not accidental formula, but rather a symbol. Could be that Lawrence Welk's mind always plans with metronomic accuracy, so that he can move ahead from task to task with minimum waste of time and energy.

I begin to ply Mr. Spaulding with questions, but before

---

* Mr. Spaulding is also Lawrence Welk's business administrator, and (since the bandleader has incorporated his business) the vice-president and comptroller of Teleklew Productions, Inc.

I gather nearly enough answers, he surprises me by announcing: "Here we are."

Is this really it? Is this the Welk home?

Subconsciously, I suppose, I must have been envisioning the kind of backdrop that the papers feature as typical Hollywood stuff—a "house of the future," sprawled with a certain casual opulence on a convenient mountainside ledge, and flanked with swimming pool or expansive terrace, with lush patio or high wall over which would tumble a profusion of scarlet bougainvillaea, or . . . or . . .

Anyway here we are, all right, and I'm looking straight at a decidedly unspectacular house, like that of any comfortably fixed John Doe. It is Mediterranean in style, and medium to smallish in proportions. There is a pretty yard —yes, the folksy noun suits—fronting it.

Whatever he is, Lawrence Welk isn't pretentious. Show for show's sake must not interest him.

But no more time for impressions of this kind. Mr. Spaulding has already deposited my bags in the house, and we are on our way again—studio bound.

"Those are the fans," Mr. Spaulding explains to me as we drive up to the place and I ask him about the long queue of people leading up to one of the doors. "They're waiting to get in and see the show. They've been there a couple of hours."

He's indicating another door, toward which I am supposed to go. We enter, and he pilots me to an auditorium seat facing the stage.

"Would you mind waiting here a moment?" he asks, and disappears.

Oh, there's Lawrence Welk. He's coming my way with Mr. Spaulding. He's taller than I thought he was—proba-

bly close to six feet. He doesn't look that tall on television.
Maybe it's that impressive breadth of shoulders which
makes him seem stockier on the screen—but then I should
have remembered that TV always does make people look
heavier than they actually are.

Now we're being introduced, and Lawrence is greeting
me with: "It is so nice to have you with us."

There's a rather stiff bow, and a slight accent to go with
the words, which together with the plural "us" seem to me
a trifle stilted and formal. What was that comment of a
friend of mine back home? "He's like a German drill-
master."

But no—on the heels of that thought comes another
pushing itself forward as an absolutely certain insight—he's
shy.

Our encounter is brief. There are technicians, stagehands, and all sorts of people milling about, and one of
them is trying to attract Lawrence's attention. He excuses
himself and moves away.

There's a sudden noise. I turn in my seat. The crowd I
had noticed at the entrance is being admitted. They pile
in eagerly, their faces rapt with expectation. They have a
good look—the look of plain, honest, conservative folk. But
I watch them only a few minutes before I turn back to the
stage. I don't want to miss any eleventh-hour preparation
that might be going on there.

Strangely, it is quiet. In fact there seems to be an un-
natural hush. What's this? Suddenly I am conscious of tension crackling in the air like electricity. As the minutes tick
away, it grows in intensity, almost, it seems, to the breaking point. The musicians, their nerves tauter than the

strings of their instruments, are waiting for the show to begin.

But there's a rustle. "That's the public relations manager," explains Mr. Spaulding, who has come back and taken a seat beside me.

This man, Ralph Portner, is greeting the audience with a little speech, and instructing them about the dancing on the show and about applause.

He steps aside as Lawrence appears, and a wave of fervid clapping sweeps through the house. The bandleader waits for it to pass. But now he is talking, welcoming his fans personally. Behind him and to the left stands Myron Floren. Lawrence beckons to him, asks him to play the accordion, and says to the crowd: "Would any lady here like to polka with me?"

Would anyone! At his word a number of women crowd toward the stage. Some bashful and wistful, others urgent and pushing. Lawrence is taking them as they come. Apparently he intends to give as many as possible a whirl.

"The gals sure love that!" I hear a man behind me commenting.

And it's a good idea, too, because it has eased the tension. There's that Welk smile that I've remarked on television. This is the first time I've seen it real life.

But the music stops, and the dancing ends. As though a switch had been thrown, the smile goes off; Lawrence could not be concentrating more seriously as he turns back to his orchestra. The tension which had been momentarily slackened is now drawn tighter than ever. Why, I'm even conscious of my own breathing, and my racing pulse.

The public relations man is stepping forward again. He holds out his arm. What's he doing? I see: he's marking off the passage of the remaining seconds before the show. It's like the ritual of a weird, archaic cult, and it seems interminable. I can't breathe, and I'm getting goose bumps.

Oh, at last! The outstretched arm and pointed finger of the high priest is giving the signal: "We're on the air."

Was it I sighing audibly with relief?

Chapter 3

♫

"The Music Goes 'Round and 'Round"

The show over at seven o'clock, California time, we are on our way again. We go to the Ontra cafeteria for a quick bite of dinner, and then hurry on to the Aragon Ballroom in Ocean Park. Across the marquee of this building, colored lights spell out: "LAWRENCE WELK AND HIS CHAMPAGNE MUSIC."

On the bandstand here Lawrence Welk seems a subtly different person from the one he had been in the studio. Now beyond the camera's rude stare, he is at ease and can give himself wholeheartedly to the music. Even when he isn't dancing, his feet move in rhythm to the beat. Indeed, his whole body seems sensitively vibrant, as though every tone passes through it, turned antenna. But inwardly, too, he is responding to the sound waves. The vivid Welkese smile lights his face with a brightness which seems to rise not only from the patent "having a good time," but also from a deeper source, an inner bubbling spring of sheer joy in melodic sound.

Somehow in the jumble of first impressions this is connected in my mind with the term "Champagne Music." It is apt in more ways than one. It suits the music, yes, but it also suits Mr. Music Maker himself. He has an effervescent joy and energy as burbling as the festive wine and just about as exhilarating to all who come within his range.

While I'm watching him, it dawns on me that I am in the midst of a small crowd. Mr. Spaulding, faithfully at my side, assures me: "That's nothing unusual. There's always a bunch of people around the bandstand. They just stay here, looking up at Lawrence and the band."

A girl waves a paper at him: "Please, Mr. Welk, I'd love your autograph. I'm all the way from Baltimore."

As he takes the paper from her, he says a few words to her and then to many other people who press toward him. His manner is casual and friendly, but at the same time dignified.

What is he saying? There's a certain phrase he keeps repeating. I edge a few feet closer. There, I've caught it. He's saying what he said to me earlier: "It's so nice to have you with us."

By now the "us" doesn't seem formal. I'm beginning to understand that Lawrence Welk does not think of himself apart from his associates, and the pronoun, as he uses it, refers to "the boys," and to himself only as one of them. He takes no credit for *his* orchestra being good; it is "the boys" who "play real wonderful."

And Mr. Spaulding is telling me that Lawrence recognizes talent anywhere any time. Here at the ballroom he often allows music-minded customers to the stand to direct for a while, or he will put the microphone at the disposal of an aspiring singer who may hope that Welk recognition will lead to a better job.

"He hired Jim Roberts, the tenor, that way," my mentor continues. "One night Jim showed up here at the Aragon, hoping to arrange for an audition. Lawrence said: 'How about right now?' A letter of introduction or pull doesn't mean much to Lawrence. He just looks to performance, and anybody he can help along he does. He particularly likes to give the young ones a boost."

And Lawrence's unorthodoxy goes further. I notice he stirs up interest from time to time by dancing with a customer, and he also invites ladies in the crowd to the bandstand to choose one of the boys for a partner. If the entire orchestra is thus simultaneously whisked away to the floor, Lawrence picks up his accordion or turns to the organ and plays a solo.

Any wall between patrons and performers has long since crumbled, and the affair has taken on the air of an informal, private party where everybody knows everybody.

Now the music comes to an end for a short intermission, but Lawrence has no chance to leave the bandstand. Autograph seekers besiege him.

"The way he's smiling you'd think he was enjoying himself," I comment.

"And this goes on from 8:30 to 2 A.M.," Mr. Spaulding reminds me.

"How do you stand it?" I ask Lawrence as soon as I can work my way toward him.

"Oh, the folks are real nice," he beams.

"But doesn't this ever get you down?" I gesture toward the crowd still clamoring for autographs.

Before he can answer, some girl grabs his arm and tries to pull him from the bandstand. I overhear what she's saying: "You're old enough to be my grandfather, but I want to dance with you anyhow, so I can tell the folks back home about it."

Apparently Lawrence is amused by her remark, tactless

—and indeed untrue. Grinning broadly, he promises her a dance.

"Saturday night is more hectic than other nights," Mr. Spaulding tells me. "That's when the crowd is largest."

"It looks like it's made up of a pretty good class of people, though," I comment. "Better than usually frequent a public ballroom, isn't it?"

"I should say it is," Mr. Spaulding affirms. "And on the nights that Lawrence holds his weekly dance contests, it's even more impressive."

But here's Lawrence again, and I have a question to ask him. "With two shows a week, will you be able to continue indefinitely playing here at the Aragon?"

His answer proves that he would like to. "Only when we're close to folks like here at the ballroom can we know what they want, and that's the most important thing to us. It helps the TV show and it's worth the extra time, effort, and work."

Work—I want to know about that, too. "Now that you've attained the heights in your profession, can you ease off at all?" I inquire.

Lawrence smiles as he replies: "I never worked harder in my life. Each step upward seems to bring more responsibility and more work. Even back on the farm, I didn't put in more hours, and——"

We are interrupted. The "music goes 'round and 'round." I won't have another chance to speak with Lawrence tonight. I mention to Mr. Spaulding that I am tired, and he offers to take me "home," to the Welk house.

I move back toward the bandstand, hoping at least to say a brief "Good night," and that's about all I can squeeze in.

Ah—now for bed.

The time is around midnight. What a day! I'm going to get beneath those covers in a jiffy for sure. But Lawrence Welk—he's still out there; he will still be making music till the wee hours, and hadn't he said in parting: "See you for ten-o'clock church in the morning"?

Chapter 4

"Hi, Ho, Hi, Ho, It's Off to Work We Go"

It is early morning and the beginning of a proper work week. Notebook in hand, I'm ready to interview any man, woman, or child who can tell me about Lawrence Welk.

But I would prefer to start with the subject himself. There he is in the breakfast room. He's wearing a tan, open-necked, short-sleeved shirt, which is actually only a few shades darker than his tanned skin. Despite those long hours on the bandstand he must find time for the outdoors.

Maybe he will choose the grounds in the rear of the house for our literary get-together. But no, he's leading the way into the small room to the left of the living room. It's the sort of cozy nook, usually called a den, but one which the Welks might just as aptly call a music room or library. In one corner stands an artist concert organ, and along one wall, bookshelves. The chairs are upholstered with leather, and they indicate by a sturdy masculine-type comfort that here is Lawrence's special domain.

I remark this casually to Lawrence, and I am rather surprised at the response I evoke. Immediately he launches into an earnest little speech, explaining that Mrs. Welk, Fern, decorated the entire house, "which is right, because," he avers, "the woman has to make the home. She *is* the home—the center and heart of the family."

"And the man is head?" I ask.

He nods seriously. "The man has to take the responsibility for big decisions—and especially about business conditions. He has to do the planning and lead the whole family. That's the way it's meant to be."

What sort of a character is this? Is he a rigid stickler for . . . I dismiss the half-formed thought, as he gives me a disarming little-boy smile and adds: "Fern is real wonderful. She's a real wonderful wife and mother. I only hope I do my part right."

I murmur: "I see," but about all that I do see clearly at this point is that interviewing Lawrence Welk is not going to be like interviewing more conventional mortals. I don't know what to expect next.

And I thought that I had come to Hollywood prepared for anything!

But whatever I was prepared for, and regardless of the kind of man I found Lawrence Welk to be, I had taken for granted that we would begin our interviews by discussing his career, and by my taking notes derived largely from the questions I'd ask him. I came provided with the usual stock in trade: To what do you attribute your success? Have you always had a bent for music? Tell me about your early life, and what determined you to take up this profession? And so on.

Now, I'm not sure that I'll bother with the rigmarole. I make a few tentative approaches of a different sort. No matter what I say, Lawrence takes off from there on a flight of his own, which may carry him into a little speech, frequently with moral overtones, but always with a touching earnestness, and with the (I must use the word) sweet, bashful smile.

Well, so much the better to have him talk in his own way. Then not only will events come out one by one, but, more important for my aim, the man himself will take form.

Meanwhile, my eyes are straying to the bookshelves to scan the titles up there. I see few general topics represented, little history, biography, or fiction. In fact two types of reading matter comprise the whole lot: religious books and what—for lack of a better term—could be called success books, that is, essays on how to succeed in business.

Turning back to Lawrence, I find myself blurting out: "I guess you're pleased that I'm writing this biography because it might help you publicity-wise?"

It is an unusual opening for any line of questions, but his reply, spoken with sincere concern, is much more unusual. Leaning forward, and making a steeple of his strong, capable-looking, tanned hands, he says solemnly: "I want a book that will help folks. I've learned a great deal in show business, and when you've had some share of success, people are likely to listen to you, and even imitate you. I wish I could find a way to pass on what I might know about avoiding certain troubles and dangers."

"What, for instance? What troubles and dangers?"

"Well, for one thing, when we have a little success, it's so easy to be bossy with folks, and to think we're perfect. That's very dangerous."

As he goes on talking, I realize that the man is a moralist, and a rustic sage, but above all he is a missionary, naïve, perhaps, but sincere, bursting with a humble desire to share with his fellow man precepts and ideas he has found useful in his own life.

If his thoughts are not original in the sense that they have never been expressed before, I'm sure that they are original for Lawrence, in the sense that they were produced by dint of his own hard pondering on life as he has lived it.

And since he has worked to dig out his truth, he sees it as a priceless find, a shining nugget of wisdom, to be grasped tightly. In his eyes it is not hand-me-down words, covered with the dust of old expression, and stale with the smell of musty books, to be taken for granted or disregarded entirely.

I find his enthusiasm catching, his earnestness impressive. For instance, when he confides to me as though it were a priceless secret known only to the initiated: "I've found a way to have a real smooth life. It isn't by doing what we feel like, or what comes first. It's by doing what's right," the concept strikes me with greater impact than Dante's poetic expression of the same idea: "In His will is our peace."

Or when he explains gravely: "You can bring out the best in other folks by a few nice words, better than all day long ordering them around," it makes a deeper impression than reading Francis de Sales's "More flies are caught by a drop of honey than a barrel of vinegar."

Of course I can see even this early in the game that Lawrence Welk, with his rather cumbersome speechifying and his twists of phrase, is no fashioner of pithy epigrams, nor is he adroit at tossing off the witty bon mot. Indeed his very vocabulary is limited, so that he must often repeat words; already I am beginning to label them in my mind with the quasi-trademark, Welk Words. Then like a schoolboy, anxious to be letter perfect, and trying so hard that he becomes self-conscious, he stumbles occasionally and makes mistakes. But these quirks not only personalize his speech, they also enlist, I find, a sort of affectionate sympathy.

After all, he was brought up in a German-speaking community, where at church, at school, or on the street he heard very little English. He was twenty-one and on his way in the "music business" before he made any concerted effort to learn English.

Incidentally, that fact answers the question many people ask: Why does Lawrence Welk have an accent? And the answers to more important questions are piling up around me. Let me get to them.

♫

Chapter 5

"Down on the Farm"

"How did a man comparatively unknown nationwide become overnight 'the hottest thing on TV'?" I put that question to one of Lawrence's henchmen.

The answer cuts me down to size. Only people who don't know the facts call Lawrence's success an overnight phenomenon. The name Lawrence Welk had been a byword in the Midwest for years before the band went to California. Lawrence's popularity had grown at a sure, steady pace until it reached the heights where network TV was almost inevitable. If, to greenhorns like myself, Lawrence Welk may seem to have emerged abruptly, that's only because of the nature of the television medium. Through the simultaneous flick of millions of dials it operates on a new level.

"For nearly thirty years, I've been working up real slow," Lawrence himself tells me. "It has to be that way. If you build fast, you fall fast."

"I'd like to hear about those thirty years," I prod. "'They say' that you've had a regular Horatio Alger life, with plenty of tough struggles, and harrowing disappointments to overcome. How did you get to the top?"

"If a man works hard, and lives right, he can't hold himself back—not in this country," Lawrence assures me.

"That's a glowing testimonial for our economic system, but," I persist, "it doesn't explain why your band is way out in front of the rest. Don't the others work hard?"

"Maybe. But hard work in the wrong direction gets us nowhere. There are orchestra leaders who are mostly interested in a good word from the critics; they try to impress a few fellow musicians, and are more anxious to put on a show than to keep a steady beat—all of that is wrong. The audience should come first. We should try to please them."

"How about describing Champagne Music for me in your own words?" I suggest.

"Well, our music is simple. I'm strong for simple arrangements. We try for a melody that everybody can pick out, and we try to have an easy-to-follow rhythm. Of course we want a nice pleasant harmony, and a volume that's not too loud—none of that earsplitting stuff."

"And the sparkling quality which makes its name so appropriate? How do you achieve that?"

"We try for a light bubbly feeling with our instrumentation and arrangements, but here . . . I have something that George Thow wrote. George plays the trumpet in our band. He tells how we get the effect we want."

Lawrence handed me a sheet of paper from which I read: "Lawrence Welk relies on the delicate woodwinds —flutes and clarinets—rather than on saxophones; on muted brass as against the blaring 'open' sound; on muted violins and a great deal of accordion and organ. The reeds concentrate on a graceful style which consists largely of triplets or dotted eighth and sixteenth notes. The brass play staccato for the most part. The violins play melody or obbligato as the music calls for. The organ and accordion supply variety and tonal color. Underlying these several sections and furnishing a foundation and definite beat is the rhythm section of drums, bass viol, guitar, and piano."

"I don't know whether I understand it all," I comment, returning the paper to Lawrence. "All I know is that you've hit on something that the public loves—and should I add, you've also hit the jackpot."

"We made money after a while. But that's a funny thing: some fellows talk about that, saying we're 'commercial' as though it were wrong for us to make money and pay our musicians regularly. What's wrong with making money if you do it fair and square? You supply jobs for lots of folks, and you improve their situation as well as your own. I wonder if a lot more bandleaders wouldn't make big money if they were patient enough, instead of trying for short cuts to success."

"Few leaders have your ability to sense what the public wants. I've been told that you have a sixth sense, which amounts almost to clairvoyance. You always know just what will go over."

"It's not a sixth sense. As I said, I just try to please our audience . . . decent people, the kind of folks that have been my friends and neighbors all my life."

"If you had to name a few people who helped you along the rugged path to success, who would they be? Mrs. Welk, maybe?"

"Fern understood what I was aiming at, and she knew I couldn't be happy without music. Some wives can kick up a lot of fuss about the music business. Mostly we musicians have to be on the road a lot, so it's harder to have a home. Always Fern kept a real home for me to come back to. Then my children—well you know Shirley, and Donna, and Larry. It was easier for me to stay away from different kinds of temptation because I wanted to be a proper father to such grand kids. Steering clear of a bad life, though I didn't do it for that, of course, helped me pay attention to the music business and get ahead in it."

"And your parents?" I inquired. "Did they encourage your musical talent, and help you launch a career?"

Lawrence grinned. "Maybe they encouraged music, but they didn't like my career—not in the beginning. There was a time when my father would have given a year's wheat crop to see me a farmer. He was scared I might go wrong if I spent my life in and out of dance halls. But my parents did help. They taught me important things. I believe in those things. What a man believes in, and what he is, has a lot to do with the kind of success he makes. Do you want to hear about my life on the farm?"

"I want to hear about your whole life," I assure him.

Out where the prairie meets the sky in the broadest of arcs, and the lazy clouds drift slowly over the fertile earth, lie the billowing wheat fields and the sod house.

The place holds many clues to Lawrence Welk's character and to his success. Actually, in order to understand anything clearly about Lawrence Welk, the man, it is "elementary" to go back to the site of his boyhood and play the sleuth.

The life there was "pretty hard," as Lawrence says, but he adds quickly: "My parents didn't come to America to find easy conditions. They came to find freedom. And they were willing to work for it."

Their native land was Alsace-Lorraine, that territory tugged and torn at by German-French rivalry. In 1878, after the Franco-Prussian War, they left the place behind rather than bend their erect backbones beneath Prussian militarism and regimentation.

"But they didn't come straight to America," Lawrence explained. "A whole group of Germans went to Odessa in the southern Ukraine district of Russia. My father, Ludwig, was just a boy then. He went with his parents, like my mother went with hers."

As soon as young Ludwig found out that they had not bettered their lot by the move, and that a goose-stepping soldier's life was also prescribed in the land of the czars, he set his sights on the far horizon—on America, "the land of the free."

"Of course, it took a few years to find a way to get here," Lawrence pointed out. "Meanwhile, my father and mother got to know and like each other real well, and they were married."

It was in the year 1892 when the two, Ludwig and Christina (now with another group of emigrants, derived from the original Alsatian group), set out for the New World.

When they reached this country, although Christina was five months pregnant, they, along with their countrymen, immediately pushed west. Out there homesteading was still open to those stouthearted enough to tackle the job of clearing the ground and building from scratch. At length the little band of pioneers reached, and settled on, a broad strip of fertile land in North Dakota, where they built themselves sod shelters before the cold weather set in. The little town which gradually grew up adjacent to their farms was called Strasburg. Though the spelling was

different from that of the Alsatian Strasbourg or Strass-
burg, the old-world city was evidently in their minds.

But what did Ludwig and Christina have with them to
set up housekeeping? Did they bring any possessions?

The sole notable treasure that Papa and Mamma Welk
carried with them during the long, long trek from Southern
Russia, across Europe, over the wide seas, and throughout
the arduous wagon trail winding up mountains and down
plains, was . . . but let Lawrence tell it: "Along with the
family Bible, they had an accordion," he says. "It was supposed to have been handed down from a blind ancestor,
who was a kind of strolling player."

Talk about clues!

If children of such parents weren't born with music bred
in their bones, it would be odd indeed. Providence waited,
however, for the sixth child before it produced the accordion lover and player who is Lawrence.

"I was only about three years old," he recalls, "when I
began trying to reach the keys and pump the bellows of
our old-fashioned pump organ."

He continued to reminisce about the long winter evenings. "When the chores were done, music was everything," he declared. "My older brother played, and I
wanted to do what he was doing. Papa used to help me
'play' too by guiding my stubby fingers on the buttons of
the old-fashioned accordion. At the same time, he'd be
pumping the bellows for me.

"Later when I was older, we'd have little concerts. While
Papa played the accordion, John, my oldest brother, would
play either the violin or the clarinet, and I would chord
along on the old-fashioned pump organ. That was good

training in rhythm for me. Maybe it helps me today. Anyway, we had real wonderful times."

Apparently the exquisite delight of those evenings and other, similar ones lingers nostalgically in Lawrence Welk's memory. He drew more word pictures.

There are the whole family, four boys, four girls, father and mother, gathered around the potbellied kitchen stove, which ruddies their faces in its warm glow. John picks up the accordion and plays snatches of melody. Suddenly Papa pulls Mamma to her feet, and whirls her about in a waltz, Mamma laughing and protesting: "*Ach*, Ludwig, you tease! I'm not a girl any more."

After a few minutes he gives her an affectionate squeeze and releases her. Now, it is his turn to play the accordion. He chooses first a hymn and then some folk songs from the old country, while the children, their treble voices ringing clear, sing on and on.

Let the blizzards sweep from the north, let the snow pile up beyond the window sills to shut them away from all the world, let the wind unleash its demoniacal fury in the night, let the wolves howl eerily from the dark clump of trees just over the swell of the fields—still the cold, the isolation, and the weird sounds were forgotten.

"Our family had so much together," Lawrence declared.

Yet there must have been times, especially when the older folk were away helping some neighbor, when those wolves sounded ominously close, and Lawrence admitted: "It did give us a creepy feeling to hear them. I never quite got used to them."

Also Lawrence can practically relive other nights when he snuggled down under the patchwork quilts to lie there quaking with dread (somewhat deliciously heightened by boyish imagination, no doubt) as he thought of the nearby Indians on the reservation. Occasionally a few of them, off on a drinking spree, would rove the farms, curious, perhaps, as had been their ancestors, about these strange pale-faced settlers.

After Lawrence recalled this memory, he paused a moment, before he went on, to present arguments that he probably used to bolster his morale in the long-ago. "But our walls were safe and thick—two or three feet thick. They kept us real snug."

He further explained that those thick walls kept the warmth inside during the winter, and made it cool "like air-conditioning" in summer. And the house was "pretty good size with an upstairs and all." The walls were whitewashed and spotless. "We kids loved it when we were snowbound and couldn't get out, but," he added hastily, "not because the place was nice and comfortable, but because we could usually count on a blizzard lasting three days, anyhow. Three days to make music before we could go back to work!"

They timed their holiday—as they did other periods, for that matter—by the sky visible through the upper part of the window. When there was grayness outside, that meant a sun behind the fuzzy whirl of snowflakes; when there was blackness that meant night. They didn't have to consult clocks to tell the hour or the passage of days.

This was an interval of strange, secret enchantment, beyond time and outside the workaday world. No wonder that winter, harsh though it was, quickens Lawrence's heartbeat even as he tells about it now.

Moreover, though summer was easier, it had its capri-

cious moments. In fact Lawrence said: "All seasons have
their bad conditions."

Sometimes there were sandstorms, prairie fires, plagues
of grasshoppers, or even more frequently hailstorms.

"I can still remember," Lawrence remarked, "the sick
feeling that used to come over us when we would have to
stand by helplessly and watch a hailstorm."

A few minutes of severe hail could tear a wheat crop to
shreds, and destroy the months of patient, backbreaking
toil which had gone into sowing and cultivating it.

"But it was all part of the life," Lawrence stated. "There
were good times and there were bad. We did the best we
could."

Even when the wheat crop failed, they were not entirely
dismayed. "You learned to get along somehow," Lawrence
pointed out. "We had chickens and we sold eggs. We had
a cow, and there was milk. Then Papa, whose family in
the old country were all blacksmiths, earned a little money
shoeing horses."

Apparently the Welks never felt sorry for themselves, for
Lawrence explained: "Our parents taught us that life was
meant to have some hard conditions. How else could we
grow strong? How else could we learn faith in God? It was
all for a purpose."

Religion was as pervasive as the air they breathed,
though he declared: "We didn't think of ourselves as religious. God was a fact like the sun. And like the sun shone
down on us, God up there was looking after us."

Prayer came almost spontaneously. "Worshiping the
good Lord, Who gave us everything we had, seemed natural, like eating, or sleeping or working," Lawrence testified,
and he added: "Mamma told us that when we tilled the

earth, and did what we should, that was a kind of prayer too—if we remembered we were working in His service."

Not that they neglected formal prayer, either. There was always a short grace before and after meals, as well as family morning and night prayers.

And churchgoing, too, was part of the pattern. In Strasburg, about three miles from the farm, stood the church of St. Peter and Paul's. Come Sunday, Papa donned his stiff collar and tie, Mamma her beribboned bonnet, and the whole family their resplendent "best" to drive to town for church. The worst winter weather did not seem sufficient excuse to stay home.

"Many a time, just to begin work on a weekday morning, we had to shovel our way through real deep snow from the house to the barn, so we would do as much to get to church," Lawrence declared. "We often had temperatures of thirty to forty degrees below zero in the winter. Icicles would form on our nostrils, and even our eyelashes would get ice on them, so that sometimes, just to keep our eyes from freezing shut, we had to stop and warm them by shielding them from the cold air with our gloves. Then our fingers—they would be so stiff that it was hard to move them enough to hitch the horses to the buggy. It was awful hard, too, to get through snowdrifts, or to see more than a couple of feet ahead if snow was falling right then. But we didn't miss church."

No wonder when in later years the wide wanderings of his business made getting to church regularly on Sundays all but impossible, Lawrence Welk still didn't miss. Speaking of the era during which he played a morning radio program in Yankton, South Dakota, and evening dance bids throughout the surrounding country, he said: "Often we went right far for a Saturday-night dance, and that meant driving back to Yankton at dawn for our early broadcast. Seems like we were always pressed for time. It was stop either for church or breakfast—not both. I'd go to church. Maybe I didn't have any strict duty, traveling and all, but the home training made me feel that I should start the week out right by worshiping the good Lord. I'd get the boys who went to some diner to bring me out a bite to eat on the bus into town."

Perhaps that home training is responsible for a great deal more. Perhaps it offers clues to all that follows.

♫

Chapter 6

"School Days, School Days"

The only schooling Lawrence Welk had was in the elementary grades, where he learned the ground rules of "readin', and 'ritin', and 'rithmetic." That schooling was under the auspices of the Ursulines. A few nuns of this order had come to the Dakotas from Germany, to teach children "in the mission fields," that is, in the far-flung places where religious education was not readily available. As a matter of fact, theirs was the only school in the area.

During the severe winter months, in order to save a tiny tyke the arduous going back and forth, Lawrence lived with the nuns in their little house which served as both school and convent.

"I was a kid with a lot of mothers," he describes it.

The curriculum was carried out largely in German. Though some of the Sisters understood English, they could not easily persuade the parents to have their children change abruptly to the new tongue.

Says Lawrence: "Out there on the plains, we were really apart from the rest of the world, so most everybody around just spoke their native language. None of our parents knew more than a few words of English. Anyway, the Sisters taught us our prayers and told us stories from the Gospels in German."

He further recalls that they spent long hours teaching the children the alphabet, and showing them how to form its letters on slate or paper, and he mentions that "back on those days, writing was all fancy curlicues, but we had to do it, and do it real neat. And we learned some figuring and spelling with drills and spelling bees."

But Lawrence points out: "None of these things were as important as what we learned from the Sisters' lives. Sisters live not for themselves but for other people, and they offer everything they do to God. I guess we kids didn't really think that out at the time, but some of it rubbed off on us, and it taught us a lot—about unselfishness, and unworldliness, and all."

Having given this little dissertation Lawrence paused a minute, and then added as an afterthought: "But if I talked about schoolwork only, then I'd say that the most important thing the Sisters taught us was to keep our minds on a question real steady, till we figured it out. I remember they'd tell us: 'You can play later. Now, get to work and put your whole mind on studying.' That training has helped me ever since."

So Lawrence was taught to concentrate! Obviously that did help him through the years to pick up additional education where and when he could—not from books alone, but from practical experience. Despite his skimpy four years of schooling he has indeed picked up so much education that certain institutions of learning would be more than proud to count him as an alumnus. They have proved it. The high school of Strasburg, North Dakota, recently on the *This Is Your Life* program presented Lawrence with an honorary diploma, and the University of Portland, in 1956, conferred upon him an honorary degree of Doctor of Fine Arts.

"A person who wants it will get some education, school or not," Lawrence says, just as he tells his children, whom he is sending to college: "A person who doesn't want it, and won't work for it, doesn't get much education even if he stays in school, graduates and all."

Not that Lawrence is, or ever was, an Abe Lincoln, poring over countless books by the flickering light of the fireplace. Books play an important but necessarily limited role. He explains: "Back on the farm, we were pretty tired at night after working all day in the fields. What we did read, though, we had time to think about and get the most from. Then, too, I used to get a lot from the Sunday Gospel, and the Sunday sermon. When you're outside all day looking up at the sky, it's easy to think of things like that. Have you ever noticed that lots of texts have to do with the outdoors and farm life? You know, like 'Consider the lilies of the field,' which tells us to trust God, and 'I would have gathered thy children as the hen doth gather her chickens under her wings,' which teaches us about God's love and care for His people . . . and there are lots more. I still try to think extra hard about what I read, because even now I don't have time to read as much as I'd like, and try to read steady—some every single day. Before I turn off the light and settle down to sleep at night, I get in a few minutes with a book. I can say that books have influenced the way I think more than my friends and business associates ever have. That's why I want to choose only good-quality reading."

He makes clear what he means by quality when he says:

"First things must come first. And there's nothing ahead of religious books," but at the same time he points out that he enjoys other reading too.

With all this, would Lawrence really have accelerated his career, and reached his goal sooner, had his formal education been more extensive? A girl reporter, querying him on the point, received only this answer: "I don't know. Maybe I wouldn't have worked as hard, and gotten as far, if I had begun in the music business after twelve years or so of easy life in classrooms."

Regarding strictly musical education, his attitude is probably different. He doesn't say much about it. Though he once took a correspondence course from the United States School of Music, the only time he ever saw the inside of a regular music school was when he enrolled for a course in piano tuning at the MacPhail College of Music in Minneapolis. (Incidentally he has yet to tune a piano.)

It might be interesting indoor sport to speculate as to whether musical education would have diverted Lawrence's choice of fields. Recently, having hired a group of eighty musicians for the job, he made a record album of popular melodies taken from symphonies. "I like that kind of music, too," he confesses.

Perhaps with training he might have become a Bach, Beethoven, and Brahms enthusiast. Who knows? But if he had, would he have attained a success comparable to what he has attained in dance music? Or can the two fields be compared?

Enough of this if-fy business! It's high time to find out why Lawrence left school while he was still in knee breeches. The reason hangs on an event which occurred in his eleventh year, and which marked the end of his early childhood period.

One sultry night of late summer, just at the beginning of the threshing season, he woke up with queer pains. It was, he thought, "a real bad stomach-ache." He lay awake, turning and twisting in his narrow bed, and longing for morning, when he was sure that the sharp torment, like a nightmare, would fade away. Finally, he saw through the window the faint gray of dawn, and then at last the sun, a ball of fire, flaring in the east. But strangely, there was no change. Lawrence couldn't understand it.

"It didn't seem real," he says. "In our family, folks mostly didn't get sick—aside from myself, that is. I was a kind of puny kid. But even I had never had anything like this before. I felt ashamed of my ill condition. It was threshing time. My father was counting on me along with the rest, for a share of the work. I hated to let him know how weak and sick I felt. And I didn't want my big brothers to know either. They kidded me enough as it was."

When he went down to breakfast that morning he scarcely dared to speak to anybody, lest he give away his secret. He need not have been so fearful. There were chores to be done—and in a hurry, since outside hired help would soon be arriving to lend a hand with the big threshing job. Who could take the time to notice the pale, hollow-eyed boy leaning up against the wall, trying to make himself inconspicuous?

Happily breakfast was a swift affair, and then came the signal for Lawrence to be on his way.

"My job, the one Papa told me to do, was to drive one of the wagons, hauling wheat from the threshing machine to the storage bins. I started work all right, but in the barn some of the workers did mention that I had a green look, and asked how I felt."

Lawrence kept tight-lipped and shrugged off their questions. But it wasn't long before excruciating pain doubled him into paroxysms that could no longer be ignored.

In a daze he saw his father come toward him, then Brother John was off to the house for Mamma, and an indeterminate time afterward his brothers laid a faded quilt on the bare boards of one of the wagons and lifted him in on top of it.

The ride that followed was to the doctor in Strasburg. The wagon jolted along the rutted, dusty roads, and each jolt brought a jab of hot, suffusing pain. The boy clenched his teeth in an effort not to scream aloud; he balled his fists and brushed away the tears that, no matter how hard he tried to stop them, would squeeze beneath his eyelids.

Then he remembers his mother leaned over him and wiped his forehead with a hand that shook. His last reserve of stoicism crumbled and he clung to her as though his life depended upon never letting her go. Then the pain in black, sickening waves broke over him, time after time . . . after time . . .

Finally, there was one overwhelming wave, and he sank beneath it, unconscious.

♫

Chapter 7

"True Love"

When they arrived in Strasburg that memorable day, the doctor diagnosed a ruptured appendix, and ordered an immediate operation. The problem was to get young Lawrence to the hospital in Bismarck, seventy-five miles away.

The next few hours were crucial.

One of the rare cars in Strasburg was owned by a relative, a John Klein (his son Johnnie is now Lawrence's drummer), and it was a question of quickly arranging with him to drive the ill boy those seventy-five miles. Had Mr. Klein not been available, there surely would have been no hope for Lawrence.

As it was, the following weeks were anxious ones for the Welk family. The little boy lying there in the hospital cot, staring at the ceiling with unseeing, glassy eyes, seemed closer to death than to life, for peritonitis, with its devastating effects, had set in.

Lawrence, now in his fifties, does not recall much of this. He has one shadowy recollection only. "I can barely remember," he says, "getting out of bed somehow and trying, half crazy like, to crawl up the wall. Then I found strong arms around me, probably the nurse's, holding me back.

I guess that was the crisis of my illness. Afterwards I gradually got better."

Seven weeks from the day of his admittance to the hospital he was allowed to return home—with a drain in his side, and it was some months before he was on his feet again. Then for a full year weakness prevented him from returning to school, and from performing even the simplest of farm chores. The frail, lanky child would go behind the barn with the accordion. Alone there, he would play the instrument for hours at a time, though his sister Eva recalls that he usually stopped abruptly when somebody came upon him.

"I was always a little shy," Lawrence admits, "but I was even shier after my illness."

And no wonder! The long convalescence enforced seclusion. Not only was he deprived of children's companionship during the school season, but the same was true throughout vacation. His brothers and sisters were kept busy with work he could not do, and other children, if they had any scant leisure, lived much too far away for a fellow with legs still wobbly to seek out.

Music became his all. If he had liked it before, he now found that he loved it with a secret consuming passion. He admits that his very games centered about it, when he recounts: "I used to go up in the hayloft, and play—kind of silly I guess—building a violin with bits of sticks, string, and a box. I really worked hard at that contraption—harder than lots of kids work on model airplanes—until the day that one of my brothers came in without me expecting him. I dropped the thing real quick. I didn't want him to see what I was doing, and poke fun at it maybe."

This interval of sickness and solitude, since it transformed music from a social pastime into a dominant force and aim of Lawrence's life, was certainly not wasted. Today, looking back from the vantage point of middle age, he says: "I'm grateful for that year."

Did that year also mark the first glimmerings of a possible career in music? Could be. Lawrence says: "I can't remember a time when my music wasn't the same thing as my happiness, but it was probably during that year that I first began wanting to make other folks happy by playing for them. And I dreamed of audiences at the pool hall in Strasburg, and beyond . . ."

What quasi-detective ferreting out Lawrence Welk's success secrets could overlook the years 1914–15?

It ended when Mamma and Papa Welk brought up the subject of Lawrence returning to school.

"I can't go back," he told them. "The kids who used to be in my class are now way ahead of me, and the Sisters will expect me to sit with 'babies' half a head shorter than I am."

The other reason behind his reluctance to face school he did not tell them. Like a lad in love, he could not discuss it with his parents. It was that books seemed suddenly deadly dull in comparison with music. He would rather work on the farm where he would have at least an occasional chance to get off behind the barn and play the accordion.

"They were sure I'd be a farmer someday," Lawrence explains, "and they didn't think I'd need much education for that. Nobody objected real strong to my stopping."

So now the boy joined his elder brothers in the fields, and tried to do just as they did—even if he did grow weary before they were ready to quit for the day. Like them, he plowed and cultivated the land, pitched hay, and threshed grain; like them, he hurried to plant the seed as soon as frost left the hard ground in the spring, so that there would be an early crop. Such physical labor developed his muscles and it slowly changed him from a gangling boy into a husky, broad-shouldered youth. Came the day when it was no longer difficult for him to keep up with his brothers in the daily round. He too could follow his father's formula for productive farming: plow deeper, sow earlier, and keep the ground cleaner than is strictly necessary. Extra effort pays off.

But while his hands toiled and his sinews strained, where were his thoughts?

He would look out over the flat land, wind-swept and ice-sheathed in winter, dry and dusty in summer, and, feeling its very austerity and strength seeping into him, he would vow that, no matter what the cost in time, labor, or heartbreak, he would become "a real musician," he would "make folks happy."

The resolve lay always in his mind, admittedly half dormant at times, but ready at a moment's notice to spring to attention, so that many an apparently irrelevant thing reminded him of music.

"When I discovered that a pitchfork, striking in a certain way, could make a nice sound, I handled it with rhythm," he confides. "And when I discovered that beating on the empty rain barrel made a real good accompaniment to my singing, I'd be a regular 'drummer' with it."

Even a hoe or pitchfork could serve as a dancing partner as he whirled around the barn floor in time to his own humming.

"Naturally, I didn't do that kind of foolishness in front of folks," he points out.

But once he remembers looking up to see his mother at a window watching him cavorting in the field with a pitchfork partner. Her broad smile was like a warm sun, and under it some of Lawrence's shyness melted away. Music was a medium the family understood. In fact it was a medium the whole rural community understood and encouraged.

"For a country church, our choir was real wonderful," Lawrence declares, and the note of pride is not dulled by about forty years of memory. "Our leader—Max Fichtner was his name—had perfect pitch."

It was one of the joys of the Sunday holiday to listen to the choir, just as it was a reward for a day's work on the farm, to relax by the stove with the accordion.

Then somehow, in the next couple of years, John acquired a brand-new "store-bought" accordion of his own, but Lawrence, the "kid brother," was scarcely allowed to touch its shining splendor. In frustration he resolved to buy his own instrument, no matter how long it might take to save the purchase price.

"We didn't get allowances," Lawrence explains, "but Papa always told us kids that if we expected to have any special thing, or if we wanted to get ahead generally, it was up to us. We must take advantage of opportunities to earn what we could."

By hunting small game and selling the hides Lawrence scraped together a few dollars. It would take fifteen dollars to buy the accordion he wanted.

While still short of that amount, Brother John (meanwhile engaged to be married) announced one evening at supper that the wedding date had been set. A month from that day he would go to the altar with his bride.

"Right off I got an idea," says Lawrence. "And a couple of days before the wedding I told my folks that I wouldn't be going to it. They were awful surprised, and kept asking me why. I told them that somebody should stay home to take care of the chores, and it might as well be me. I had it all planned."

The morning of the nuptials dawned bright and sunny. Feeling a bit guilty, Lawrence watched the members of his family, a little stiff in their unaccustomed finery, pile into the buggy and go off to town. Then, as soon as the dust had settled, he rushed back into the house, took John's accordion from its nook, and began to play. The wedding ceremony and the festivities following it—the reception, the dancing, the beer drinking, the singing—would last all day, so all that day Lawrence played and played to his heart's content. The chores were forgotten, and only as dusk fell did he remember them. Working like fury, he managed to complete a few of the most urgent ones, before he heard in the distance the creaking of the buggy wheels indicating the family's return.

He had had his day!

"As I look back," says Lawrence, "that wonderful day stands out. It's like the time I got my own fifteen-dollar mail-order accordion. When it came my folks were kind of upset because I wanted to go on practicing long beyond the hour everybody else was in bed. Finally because Papa laid down the law, and not because I wanted to rest my aching arms, I did stop. But I was too excited to sleep."

Lying awake and looking through the window at the stars, Lawrence let his happy thoughts skip ahead to the far-off day when he would go into the big world beyond, playing music to crowds of people. Then he remembers squirming with an almost irresistible urge to get up again and practice so that he could become this great musician so much the sooner.

"It was all I could do to stay where I was," he confesses.

However, not long after that night, he received a rude setback to his hopes and dreams. The fifteen-dollar accordion could not stand the punishment he gave it; the strength he had acquired through farm labor was too much for the small instrument. In no time the reeds and shoulder straps gave way.

Back to the trap lines!

"It's a good thing I was older by then—I think about fifteen. I could earn money playing for local dances. It wasn't very long before I had saved enough to buy another instrument."

But "the course of true love never did run smooth," so something dire was bound to be in the offing. One day, while he was plowing with five horses, he noticed that one balky fellow was not doing his share of the work, and he asserts, "I got mad. I really saw some red. I can't understand the man or beast who doesn't want to do his share, and who dawdles along, expecting the world, the government, his neighbor or his teammate to take up the slack. Anyway, I stood up to lay my whip over the back of the lazy horse, and at that moment he jerked forward suddenly, the plow hit a rock, and I was thrown off balance to pitch headlong onto the ground between the horses. I landed on my left arm."

When Lawrence struggled to his feet, the arm hung strangely limp. Realizing that it was broken, big, lumbering boy of fifteen that he was, he burst into an uncontrollable fit of weeping. No doubt the pain was sharp and stinging, but those great tears that rolled down his cheeks, and splashed onto his faded blue overalls, did not spring from physical pain. They had their source in a chilling thought: "I'll never be able to play the accordion again."

Fortunately that was not the case, as Lawrence soon found out.

"While the arm was still no good for work, I figured out a way to practice. I could use my sling—or any towel sling-tied—and fasten one end around my left knee, and the other to the base side of the accordion. In this way, I could use my leg instead of my left arm for the push and pull, and I played the keys with my right hand," he explains.

Talk about tenacity! There's a word to list under clues.

But the experience also highlights another trait, or, better said, it is responsible for his acquiring another trait. Says Lawrence: "That was when I learned how bad it is to be impatient, like I was with that horse, and ever since I have tried to meet all conditions real calmly and use self-control."

Another success clue? Probably.

Then, under the heading of characters in the mystery story, might well go the name of the man who soon appeared upon the scene. He came to Strasburg a year or so after the accident.

This fellow, Tom Guttenburg, a traveling accordionist, carried with him, not the push-button type instrument, but a large piano-accordion.

"I didn't know that anything could be so wonderful as that instrument!" Lawrence declares. "Whenever my parents would let me get away, I'd go to town to listen to this

Guttenburg. As much as I loved dancing, I wouldn't get off my chair while he played. I'd just sit there watching his every move."

Then Lawrence tells of the time that Tom Guttenburg laid down his accordion, and during a short intermission stepped from the stage: "I crept up and stroked the keys kind of soft, until I heard a voice behind me."

The visiting accordionist's wife, Mrs. Guttenburg, made Lawrence jump with her words: "Young man, what are you doing? Take your hands off that accordion. It's not yours."

"That hurt real bad," Lawrence admits today. "I felt shamed to be called down like that, and besides I didn't like being told that the fine accordion wasn't mine. I knew that too well already, and to be told it was like rubbing salt on wounds."

Yet from that day forward, when Lawrence thought of the future and of his secret dreams of stirring great crowds with music, he had visions of a like instrument in his own hands.

But the dream soon became more than a dream, and the vision more than a vision. There had to be a plan, some ordered way to work toward the fine acquisition, which Lawrence decided must be the first item, or the first step in his career. He could not afford to spend time sighing and hoping. He had to do something.

"Nothing is luck with me," Lawrence says. "Always I have figured, and planned, and worked toward something, always toward a definite next step."

But what could he do in this case? The piano-accordion cost all of four hundred dollars. Though his parents had some small savings, Lawrence could never ask for a staggering sum like that. It was as much as, if not more than, the family earned on the farm in a year.

As Lawrence mulled over his problem, he recalled certain fears and preachments of his father's. He remembered that whenever he broached the subject of leaving the farm and making a career of music, he was told: "Music is fine for enjoying yourself, or playing a waltz for your neighbors, but to make a living . . . *ach*, that's another kettle of fish! Let's not have any more nonsense about it. Besides you're too young to decide what you want to do the rest of your life. A few more years here and you'll see that it's best to settle down on the farm, and work the land like other sober, decent folks."

In the light of words like these an audacious scheme formed in Lawrence's mind. He could but try it. He went to his father armed with a proposition: "I've been talking about leaving the farm, to make my living in the music business. But I will promise to stay on the farm, working as hard as I can for the next four years until I'm twenty-one years old. What's more, during that time, I'll turn over to you every cent I make playing at parties, weddings, and dances, if . . ." He paused as the awful gravity of his father's decision bore in upon him, but finally he added with a rush: "If you'll buy me a four-hundred-dollar piano-accordion right now."

Not speaking for several moments, the elder Welk looked thoughtfully at his eager son, then, furrowing his brows, he answered slowly: "I'll think it over."

Chapter 8

♫

"Don't Fence Me In"

"*Ja*—go ahead. Order the accordion you want." Ludwig Welk, paterfamilias, had spoken. Lawrence was to have the desideratum.

The boy's mind did not and could not grasp anything else, although his father went on talking: "I only hope that with a few years on the farm, you'll come to your senses and see that you belong here. When you're twenty-one, you'll have 160 acres as your share of the land. And the life of a traveling musician isn't for you. It would take you into all sorts of shady places, and believe me, Son, it would endanger your immortal soul."

The homily and the offer of property were wasted.

"I made out the order for the accordion and sent it off," says Lawrence, "and the only thing that worried me was the waiting. It took so long for the instrument to come."

While he waited, time stood still. It was as though those days were lifted from life. Until the accordion arrived at the freight station, nothing mattered. Lawrence went about like a robot, making mechanical motions in the performance of routine tasks. Only late afternoon of each day brought him respite; then he would return to the business of living, long enough to hitch the wagon up, go into town, and inquire if a package had arrived for Mr. Lawrence Welk.

Hope was deferred again and again. There were times when, driving home with no accordion beside him, the yearning and frustration within him were almost a physical pain—an aching lump rising in his throat to choke him.

When the instrument did come at last, his hands trembled so much he could scarcely unbox it.

"I really thought it was the most beautiful thing in the whole world. It even had rhinestones in it!" That's about all Lawrence can say to characterize it, and as for describing his own elation—well what words could the most eloquent find for that!

However, it was clear that, although the fifteen-dollar instrument had seemed splendid, this new paragon surpassed it a thousand times over. It transported him into a beatific bliss, not far from the portals of heaven.

"That evening I played straight through dinner, and on until long after the rest of the family were in bed," he admits. "Then the next morning, I crept from my room at about four o'clock to go to the barn, where I'd be out of earshot and not disturb anybody with some more playing."

Three days later he was hired for a dance in Bichlers Hall, the poolroom which (by the simple expedient of pushing the pool tables aside to make dancing space) doubled on Saturday nights for ballroom. That engagement was the beginning of a long series.

"There were weddings, barn dances, and name days to play for," he says. "Name days are the days we celebrate the feast of a person's patron saint. They meant big times to the folks of our town."

But often he went beyond that town. He went to other

towns at a distance where walking was out of the question.
"Then Papa let me take the buggy," Lawrence explains.
"And each of us boys had either a horse or a pony to ride
and to care for. I had a pony, so transportation was no
problem. I even rigged up a contraption in the back of the
buggy to hold my accordion."

On these playing dates he sometimes teamed up with
the pianist and choir leader of the perfect pitch, Max
Fichtner, and sometimes he appeared alone with his accordion. In either event there was seldom a set fee.

Pass-the-hat took care of the musicians, and pay ranged
from as little as $1.50 per night to as much as $100 to $150
for a three-day wedding.

Every cent went to Papa Welk.

It was a strenuous life. During the wedding festivities
there was practically no letup, from the opening strains of
the wedding march on the first morning to the last waltz,
schottish, or polka on the third night.

"Many a time, I'd finish with my left wrist bleeding from
the chafing of the accordion strap," he says. "The skin on
that wrist is just like leather now."

And even without weddings the life wasn't exactly easy,
with work in the fields by day and music by night whenever possible. During harvest and threshing time, he often
had very few hours' sleep. He played until one o'clock for
a dance, and was up again around four.

In training for the future?

"I used to get awful tired," Lawrence admits in one of
his prize understatements. "Maybe even my health got a
little weak during that time."

And yet he didn't slow down. Apparently such an idea
never occurred to him. It was foreign to his way of think-

ing, though the spending money given him by Papa Welk didn't rise with increased earnings.

The first invitation to play "far away" came from Ipswich, a town one hundred miles distant. This expedition meant the train, not the buggy. Also the new venture entailed one night away from home. "My parents didn't want me to go at first," Lawrence recalls, "but they finally gave in, because John and his wife lived in Ipswich, and I could stay with them."

The boy felt that he had turned the corner into manhood when he set off on his own for that dance, and he was in the best of spirits and playing fettle when the dance was in progress. The guests seemed to share his good humor, and nobody wanted to stop dancing at the magic stroke of midnight, nor, for that matter, did they want to stop at one o'clock or later.

The young musician could not have been more obliging. He played on and on as long as his customers clamored for encores, which was around 2 A.M.

Such an hour was unheard of in the town of Ipswich. Festive occasions notwithstanding, "decent" folk there went to bed at twelve or before.

"If I knew this, I didn't think about it while I was playing, and," he adds, "maybe I never would have thought about it except for what happened the next morning."

The next morning Lawrence went to church, and there was a long sermon, lasting "at least an hour," and every word, he was sure, was meant just for him. (If his parents heard about this, it would be the end of his musical career.) The priest, looking straight at him, spoke of the devil who came to town in sheep's clothing, and kept the people dancing and prancing into Sunday morning.

Said "devil" took the next train available to go back home.

But this was not the worst of his experiences. Once he was playing for a barn dance in Hague, another rural North Dakota town, when he received more than verbal blows.

A group of traveling construction workers, working in the vicinity, decided to look in on a dance. Naturally the local belles were only too pleased to have the stag line augmented, but the local swains were correspondingly displeased. This led to a fracas between the home-town males and the outsiders, and Lawrence soon found himself playing to an empty dance hall, while through the open windows could be heard the clash of battle going on outside.

Curiosity urged him to run downstairs from the hayloft "ballroom" and step outdoors to see how things were going.

"Well, I stepped outdoors, all right," he recounts, "but I didn't see how things were going. One of the fellows— I never knew who it was—must have thought I was a rival. Anyway, the minute I went through the doorway, I went down. He had hit me over the head with something awful heavy—a brick maybe. It felt like it."

Today Lawrence still bears a scar.

Yet nothing whatever during those years dampened his hopes of leaving the farm and becoming a full-time musician. Every day the vision of life with music grew and expanded; every day his excitement mounted. He would often look out over the strange Midas-touched sea of billowing wheat stretching to the edge of his known world, and he would wonder with a skip of heartbeat what lay ahead for him. "Out there" was another world, a different world—his for the conquering.

Or he would lie awake in his bed and look through the window at the mysterious stars in the black woolly sky and tell himself: "Those same stars shine down on big cities like Chicago, and New York. Someday . . . someday . . . I'll play in places like that."

Then he would close his eyes while the blissful thought inundated every corner of his brain with rapturous joy, and the night sounds, the thousands and thousands of insects humming in the summer stillness, sounded to him like an orchestra of the far future.

With such dreams to nourish his spirit the pleas and sermonizing of his father did not shake his resolve. However, he could no longer ignore them, and often he was involved in argument trying to explain his position.

"It's the only kind of life I want," he would say. "I'd never be any good at farming."

"*Ach*, nonsense!" Ludwig could not understand. "You know how to work the land now. But what do you know about that other kind of life? I tell you dance halls in big cities are dens of sin."

"But I don't have to commit sin myself, because other people do," Lawrence would answer.

"Even so, you shouldn't make it harder for yourself to keep straight."

"I'm not—honestly. The carryings-on, whatever they are, won't bother me. I'm thinking about music—that's all."

"Why music? What's wrong with farming?"

Arguing in circles, they ended up each time at the starting point with neither one convincing the other. The subject wore a painful groove in both their minds.

And what about Lawrence's mother?

The boy had always felt close to her, and to hurt her

would have been much more difficult for him than to cause some disappointment to his father. She didn't say a word during the father-son discussions, but the son sensed that her sympathy, if it didn't lie entirely with him, was certainly divided. However, she couldn't soften Ludwig's attitude, and when Lawrence's twenty-first birthday did come, there were last-ditch arguments and dire predictions from the father.

"You'll never make a living at it," he said in parting.

If there were one fillip needed to insure Lawrence's success, it was precisely that final dictum.

"Tell Lawrence he can't do something, and that's the very thing he sets out to prove to you that he *can* do—and do superbly. I never saw a man who rises to a challenge with more fight." So declares Lois Lamont, his secretary on the present Hollywood scene.

At any rate, in that year 1924, his debt to his father fully acquitted, he said *"Auf Wiedersehen"* to his suddenly dearer-than-ever family—to his mother and father, to John, Louis, Barbara, Eva, Agatha, Mike, and Anne Mary—and set out from the warmly familiar sod house, to begin his career in the world beyond.

It was springtime. Every tree was putting out spritely green shoots. Violets and Johnny-jump-ups were bravely breaking through the black earth. Birds, recent arrivals from the south, chirped cheerily as they flitted about, gathering bits of straw for nest building. The world was coming alive, and the road stretched ahead to. . . . Lawrence wasn't quite sure what.

It was a new act—Act II of his life.

♫

Chapter 9

"A Wandering Minstrel I"

His career had begun!

As Lawrence took the road leading from the farm—and to Hollywood after twenty-five years of traveling—he carried with him capital of a sort, to invest in his beloved "music business."

To be sure, that capital was not in the form of coin, and nobody on earth would quip, as comedian Gil Lamb did recently: "My greatest ambition is to land a job helping to carry Welk's money." However, his intangible asset of faith was enough for him.

His face was glowing, and his heart was beating fast as he set out that morning.

Mamma Welk followed him with her eyes as long as she could. His hair was neatly parted in the middle and slicked down. He was wearing his Sunday suit, and his pointed, polished shoes, ordered from a mail-order catalogue. To her, at least, he looked like the conqueror of the world.

His immediate destination was Aberdeen, South Dakota, the nearest "big town" where he might likely find a job.

Once there, he promptly discovered his handicap. Though he had no trouble landing a job, he did have a great deal of trouble retaining one.

Never in all his life had he had a music lesson, so he had never learned to read notes: What he lacked in knowledge he made up for in enthusiasm and volume. If he wasn't good, he was loud. This didn't help.

It looked like his father's predictions were all too accurate. Properly speaking, the boy wasn't making a living.

"It was a lucky condition, for me, that there was a restaurant in Aberdeen which sold meal tickets on credit, or I wouldn't have eaten very regularly," he confesses.

Often he played for fifty cents a night, and sometimes less if no crowd showed up. But he was glad to play for anything. This not only kept his fingers nimble, but it kept him, Lawrence Welk, in circulation. Besides it taught him how to sense audience response.

Then one day he happened to run into a drummer he had known slightly, some time before. The fellow suggested that they throw in their lot together and "hit the road." Lawrence was easily persuaded. Surely greener pastures lay beyond, and, he added in relating the tale: "This fellow had a car—a runabout!"

On the back of the car they strapped the drum and accordion and set forth. Arriving in the town of Oldham, South Dakota, they saw posters proclaiming in big red letters:

MIKE GIBBS AND HIS ORCHESTRA
SATURDAY NIGHT

They needed no further hints. Immediately they looked up the bandleader and offered their services. To their delight he agreed to give them a chance, come evening.

"And I thought the folks liked me," Lawrence reminisces

with a rueful little smile, "but that night turned out to be
one of the lowest points of my life."

As he was putting away his accordion after the dance,
he heard the trumpet player say to another member of the
band: "Wow! If I had to play with that accordionist, I'd
quit the business."

Lawrence was stunned. Could he possibly be that bad?
Should he go back home and admit defeat? In the throes
of doubt no sleep blessed him that night. His private little
world lay shattered as if an A-bomb had made a direct hit.

He confides: "I couldn't bring myself to leave the music
business, but I felt terrible for a long time. And I think it
made me sort of afraid when I went to ask for jobs."

Out of work, the alliance with the drummer broke up,
and Lawrence was left alone to struggle as best he could.
If he never missed a meal in the period that followed, there
were times, as some wag put it, when he was about forty-
eight hours late for dinner. So when he had an opportunity
to go with a Chicago orchestra on tour, he didn't ask many
questions. "I was just happy that I had a job again," he
says. "And we traveled to places I'd never been. I figured
I'd be getting valuable experience."

Then he discovered that the leader had the bad habit
of failing to pay salaries. As a result, the members of the
band had a bad habit of their own: they'd quit without
notice.

Several times, when Lawrence was on the verge of walking out, the leader, realizing that the accordion filled in
for missing instruments, would urge him, with the promise
of a raise, to stay on.

"I guess I let myself get talked into it, because I was
learning to read music," Lawrence explains.

"But enough is bad enough," Lawrence says. "There came a time when I finally did quit. I just couldn't see a happy future."

However, the unsatisfactory boss had inadvertently made up for his defects by giving Lawrence an idea.

Seeing what a poor manager his former employer was, in contrast to his wise and frugal parents, proved to Lawrence that he had only to follow the prudent methods of the latter, and avoid the improvident mistakes of the former, and he would be better off by being his own boss than working for others. In short, the thought came to him: "Why not strike out on my own?"

Taking all his cash, he bought an old jalopy which would serve to carry him to various spots where he might find himself playing jobs. Then he set out alone, going in the direction of his home.

His way was studded with obstacles.

Apart from the question of obtaining bids to perform musically, there was a doubt of the old car's performing mechanically. It didn't behave very well minus oil, yet if Lawrence had to travel more than ten or twelve miles between towns, the oil would not hold out. The car's appetite was such that it had consumed every drop of the lubricant before reaching a destination.

However, oil or not, Lawrence and the car managed to limp from place to place, and in each one the young musician offered to play a night's vaudeville stand at any price. If the theater owner demurred, Lawrence had an alternate proposition ready: increase the ticket by five cents and make the additional money the accordionist's share. If that did not work, at passing restaurants, he offered to play for the patrons in exchange for his dinner.

Arriving at Aberdeen again, he decided to stop there
and look up automobile dealers. He was fortunate enough
to find one who gave him sixty-five dollars for his jalopy
on a trade-in for a new car.

As he signed the contract to pay the balance of approximately seven hundred dollars, in one year, his hand was
mighty shaky and his heart thumped. "At home, buying
on time was unheard of," he explains. "But I wasn't worried so much that I might lose the car if I couldn't meet a
payment. What scared me was losing my reputation as a
good risk. And I guess, too, I thought it was sort of dis-
graceful to try to live beyond your means."

With such an attitude, no wonder he worked so hard to
lift that debt. For the following month he slept sparsely.
Playing by night and drumming up engagements by day
left little time for the luxury of bed. Sometimes he would
land a spot playing with another orchestra for a night or
two, sometimes he did solos, and sometimes he hired men
himself to form an orchestra for an evening's engagement.
The last involved quick work indeed! When he found out
that an orchestra was wanted, he would offer to furnish
it, and forthwith rush out to hire the needed musicians,
be they one or ten, as circumstances demanded.

For Independence Day he hired an orchestra and rented
the pavilion in the nearby Scatterwood Lake area, where
an annual picnic was to be held. The pay was to be on a
percentage basis; he was to receive 60 per cent of the take.
The promoter failed to tell Lawrence in advance that there
was to be formidable competition, with a baseball game
scheduled for the same day. If the young bandleader had
known that, he would have figured out some other money-
making idea.

However, it was just as well he didn't. An unpredictable quirk turned his original plan into a veritable bonanza. This quirk had to do with the weather.

In July the weather by rights should have been sunny and warm, and a great many people, counting on that, jammed the picnic grounds and the baseball park. However, rain began to fall in the early afternoon, and persisted drearily throughout the day and evening.

At the first pelting drops the crowd made a dash for the pavilion: "Step up, ladies and gentlemen! Ten cents a dance."

The downpour made even the would-be competition of the baseball game pay Lawrence an extra dividend. "How do you like that?" Lawrence exclaims in telling about it. "Those raindrops turned out to be 'pennies from heaven.'"

Because of the holiday he had hoped for a fairly good crowd, but even so, since he was paying his musicians more than the usual rate, he expected only modest profits.

"In those days," he explains, "musicians were paid about ten dollars for a single date. Well, I figured the Fourth of July was a chance to win a reputation and to prove my band better than other local bands, so I hired the best men I could find at thirty-five dollars a day. I decided that I'd build for the future by letting a lot of folks know what I could do, even if I didn't have much money left after settling up with my musicians."

But this was one time when it was actually possible to have the cake and eat it too. Toward the "end of a perfect day" Lawrence paid his men, and found $265 remained for himself.

"In all my life, I'd never made that much money at

once," he declares, and the very memory makes his eyes glisten like those of a kid on Christmas morning.

What did he do with it all?

"I wanted lots of things," Lawrence admits, "but I couldn't have felt right about buying them. I still owed on the car."

He counted over his horde, the money he had made during the hard-working last month. That, together with the picnic money, would do it! In only one month, then, although the contract terms allowed him one year, Lawrence paid the entire price of his car.

"I knew I'd feel more like a success with darns in my socks and out of debt than I would with new socks and in debt," he explains.

As what Horatio Alger wouldn't, he wanted to show off his success to the home folks, so he headed for Strasburg and the farm to enjoy a little visit with his family. Now what would his father say when Lawrence Welk, bandleader, drove up his own car, bought and paid for?

The visit stretched into a month, and its chief recreation, of which Lawrence never tired, was to drive up and down Main Street to show off the shiny new car.

Good thing he enjoyed it so much! This vacation was one of the very few holiday times of Lawrence's whole life. And it was a quiet, restful interval before the next turn of events.

Chapter 10

♫

"America's Greatest Accordionist"

The leaves began to turn, and trees flamed gold, copper, and red on the hillsides. Fall had arrived. With it came a new briskness in the air, urging Lawrence to be on his way again.

He returned to Aberdeen, where he found an acquaintance, Art Kelly, booking entertainment for a fair in Selby, South Dakota. Ah, that spelled opportunity!

"I didn't let any grass grow underneath my footsteps," Lawrence says. "Right away, I went to see Art."

Shortly afterward came the hoped-for offer of employment—a week's engagement at the fair. Quickly Lawrence rounded up musicians and hired enough men for a small orchestra.

Before the week had passed another Kelly, George T., appeared upon the scene. One night, as Lawrence was leaving the bandstand, this Kelly tapped him on the shoulder and suggested: "How about a cup of coffee?"

Over the little oilcloth-covered table he told Lawrence about his work. Although at the moment he was with a carnival playing the fair, through the winter months, he had his own troupe, called The Peerless Entertainers. He put on a vaudeville show, followed by a dance. Soon it would be time to go on tour, to many towns including the "inland towns," that is, places beyond the railroad's reach. At this point he broke off and asked: "Would you like to join us? You could play your accordion on the show, and then after my comedy act is over, you could play for the dance. I'd pay you forty dollars a week. How does that strike you?"

It struck Lawrence as almost too good to be true. The absolute assurance of a steady income through the winter was enough to make his head spin with joy.

"But," confesses Lawrence, "I was trying hard not to act excited, and I was trying to turn the proposition over in my mind before I said yes or no."

The Irishman sat there drumming his fingers on the table a minute, then, figuring Lawrence's hesitancy as reluctance, he made a surprise move: he raised the ante, saying: "Come, man, I'll split the profits with you fifty-fifty."

Without more ado Lawrence extended his hand for a hearty clasp of acceptance. Still in his early twenties, he felt that he had made a good bargain with the man in his forties. And so he had!

"In the very first week, my share was all of eighty-six dollars," Lawrence recalls. "We'd make the weekly split by taking the money left after expenses, spreading it out on a hotel bed, and counting it into two equal piles. It was mostly in nickels, dimes, and quarters, because we charged fifty cents for adults, and twenty-five cents for children. But those coins mounted up, and soon I had a real comfortable income. I bought a diamond ring to wear, just to prove to myself how rich I was getting."

But as time went on, Lawrence found that he was receiving more than money. Old George T. was a shrewd character, with a twinkle in his eye, and a bit of salty wit to his tongue. He took the serious, intense young German under his wing, and showed him how to relax, how to have self-confidence, how to be patient with himself, and above all he taught Lawrence how to deal with the public.

He would say to the boy: "Look, kid, just you remember those folks out front are doing you a favor, paying their good money to see you, so it's up to you to give them your very best—and with a smile. Use that great big glad smile of yours."

Or he would remind young Lawrence: "Don't forget there are a lot more farmers and plain folk like you and me in the world than there are ritzy guys. Never try to be something you aren't. If the day ever comes that you make a little dough, don't go putting on airs—unless you want your old public to drop you like a hot potato."

Or he would advise: "If you don't like something, don't complain about it—especially if you can't change it. You'll get a load off your own chest by griping—sure, but at the same time you might rub the townspeople the wrong way. They're your audience, so what's the good of that?"

Added to the spoken counsel, there were the very presence and example of the older man. He was a naturally genial and kindly soul, and with him Lawrence's diffidence dwindled.

Why the boy even lost his shyness with the girls! Back on the farm he had ducked at the sight of a petticoat coming his way. Now he found he could smile at a girl, and he discovered, moreover, that she was very likely to smile back. Soon he even ventured to talk to girls in his guttural accent to find further that they answered him and that they were not averse to dancing with him. And how he loved to dance!

"He got to be a real killer with the ladies," says Kelly.

But there were some things the older man did not teach Lawrence. He didn't teach the boy to read music. On one occasion, traveling from town to town, George T. discovered to his consternation that some of the sheet music was missing. "We've left it behind at our last stop," he moaned. "We'll have to go back and get it."

"Not for me you won't," Lawrence said. "I can't read all those notes fast enough to make any difference. I just set the music up before me to make an impression. It looks good."

Kelly had a hearty laugh. All the time he hadn't known that!

"But if the kid couldn't read music, so what?" asks Kelly today. "That didn't stop him from being a wonderful natural musician. Just how many guys can do what he could —listen to a phonograph record and reproduce the arrangement? He was always great, I tell ya."

And it rather irks George, now seventy-six years old, to read magazine write-ups which speak of Lawrence's discords. "A lot of that is bunk," he declares. "I guess Lawrence started those rumors himself. He's such a modest guy he remembers his mistakes better'n anything."

On the other hand, Kelly will admit readily that Lawrence played "good and loud." He recalls with a chuckle one time when that voluminous sound precipitated a small crisis. A key man in the group complained: "I just can't take it any longer. My eardrums are about to burst. I'm quitting."

For that tight little group to lose one of its members was

close to tragedy. A quick solution to the difficulty had to be found. It was none other than to have the man stuff cotton in his ears.

And speaking of a tight little group—it was that all right. Everybody had two or more jobs. Mrs. Kelly, for instance, sold the tickets, took care of the props, and was secretary-treasurer. George T. himself did a comedy routine and played the drums; the leading lady also played the piano; the leading man had to serve as straight man for Kelly's comedy bits; the saxophonist took turns at playing the banjo, and so on.

"I had the nearest thing to a single job," Lawrence avers, "and ever since those days, I've always tried not to put all the eggs in just one basket. I've wanted my boys to be able to do a lot of things. It makes a better show."

It has been alleged that one reason why the Welk band has gone over so well on TV is its variety. There is something for everybody, whether he likes the violin rhapsodies of Dick Kesner, the clowning of Rocky Rockwell, or the sweet harmonies of the Lennon Sisters.

As Lawrence says: "George T. really taught me a lot."

Anybody compiling a list of key characters in the Lawrence Welk success story?

Nor should Alma Kelly, George's wife, be slighted. She had an important supporting role in the Welk drama. She helped Lawrence to learn English, though she says: "I never gave him any real lessons. And I don't know why Lawrence thinks I did so much. I just did what everybody else was doing. Lawrence would ask questions about how to talk, and we'd answer them, and try to help him."

Occasionally, though, some of the fellows would tease Lawrence. They would purposely use an unusual word to see what he would make of it. Some of the conversations must have been amusing goobledegook. Out of the past comes an echo. Somebody says: "I lost my bet—five dollars. Was I chagrined!"

"She grinned?" Lawrence questioned in perplexity. "I do not understand."

"Cha-grined. It means I felt awful, just about sick."

"Oh, you were sick." Lawrence was all solicitude.

"Say, have you ever had acute indigestion?" comes a response.

"What's cute about indigestion?" asks Lawrence. "I thought indigestion was a sickness you got from eating greasy fried potatoes."

"Don't pay any attention, Lawrence," Alma puts in. "They're kidding you again."

She didn't use such tactics. She patiently explained to him why a girl gave him a black look when he complimented her with: "You appall to me."

Lawrence says of Alma: "She was always so kind."

Mrs. Kelly hits upon that same word, "kind," when she speaks of Lawrence. "He should be a big success," she states. "He was always kind to everybody, so everybody wanted to be kind to him, and give him a break. I remember that he kept bringing me the nicest little presents. And he was always there when anything heavy had to be moved or lifted. He was the sweetest kid in the world."

Side by side with her opinion of Lawrence goes that of her husband. George T. says of his protégé: "He was the most conscientious and naïve kid I ever saw. When I spread my bally about his being so great, and billed him as AMERICA'S GREATEST ACCORDIONIST, he'd open his eyes in wonder, but he'd never doubt that I meant what I said. It never occurred to him that anybody would tell anything more or less than the simple truth. He didn't know about building things up for the public."

For some acts Kelly dressed Lawrence as a Spanish matador, and since on only rare occasions did the shy young man of the German accent dare to open his mouth before an audience, many of the people who came to see the show believed that Lawrence was, in truth, a Spaniard.

But if German Welk could become Spanish, Irish Kelly could become Swedish. The man did a routine called "Ole the Swede." "I was supposed to be the funny one," says Mr. Kelly, and Lawrence was supposed to be the straight man and feed me lines. But if he ever got nerve enough to say something, you know what? It was that accent of his —not my jokes—that got the laughs."

Be that as it may, Kelly's skit about the Swede was very popular in the Dakota towns they traveled, so Lawrence, envisioning further triumphs, urged his boss to give larger towns the benefit of seeing it. He persuaded Mr. Kelly to head south for Kansas, Oklahoma, and Texas.

"Did I make a big mistake that time!" Lawrence exclaims in telling about the tour. "There weren't many Swedes in the new territory, so people didn't get the dialect, or think it was funny. Besides in the South, certain religions didn't allow boys and girls to dance."

Now if the Peerless troupers needed further evidence to convince them that the tour was a failure, they received it with a vengeance. One night, opening in an Oklahoma town, they rented a hall, passed out their handbills, and had all things in readiness by the usual opening hour of 8:30.

Then just before curtain raising somebody looked into

the hall. One woman—and one woman only—comprised the waiting audience.

At two-minute intervals thereafter they would peek around the still-closed curtain hopefully, to see if anybody had joined her, but not another soul entered the place. They consulted one another in consternation. By 9:15 no more consultations were necessary for there was no choice; the show would have to be canceled.

George T. stepped before the curtain and down into the auditorium to explain this fact to the woman. She listened but did not stir. She chose to sit there and argue. She had come to the show and why shouldn't they put it on for her. It wasn't her fault if other people did not appear. Poor George explained that the troupe would not be able to do its best without the stimulus of something approximating a normal audience, and he ended with a promise: "Your money will be refunded."

He was not prepared for the woman's reply. "But I didn't pay any money. I have a yearly pass. I own this building."

Back to the Dakotas the troupe limped, their pockets not exactly jangling with cash. The next season they stuck to small towns and recouped their fortunes, until one of those blanketing northland snowstorms overwhelmed and isolated them in Bismarck.

Released at last from that white bondage, they decided to disband for the rest of the winter months while many of the roads into the little towns were impassable anyway.

George T. and his wife Alma returned to their Poplar, Montana, home, and four members of the troupe, including Lawrence, made up their minds that it might be pleasant to spend the winter in New Orleans. None of them had ever been there, and they had dreamed of making this pilgrimage to the Dixieland jazz capital. Moreover, they figured, it should be as good a town as the next for a musician "to pick up a few bucks."

Their plan was to stay through Mardi Gras.

♫

Chapter 11

"America's Biggest Little Band"

The year was 1927.

Lawrence Welk, accordion player, Art Beal, piano, Johnny Higgins, drums, and Howard Kieser, sax, turned southward and headed for New Orleans in Lawrence's car.

Progress was painfully slow. A good part of the trip they had to drive along in the wake of a snowplow, but they kept going all day and night until, about 4 A.M., they reached the town of Yankton, South Dakota. Weary and bleary-eyed from lack of sleep, they decided by quick-voice vote to stop there for a few hours' rest before going farther. They checked in at the Collins Hotel on the main street and left a call at the desk for 7:30.

Nobody realized how soon that hour would come.

When the phone rang in their rooms, Lawrence was the only one of the quartet who paid any heed. He jumped up, dressed, and packed before he discovered that the others had merely turned over in their beds and gone back to sleep.

"I was disturbed," he puts it, "so I went around to the beds and woke the boys up. But," he adds, "I really shouldn't have blamed them for sleeping late that morning."

Ordinarily Lawrence considers tardiness "real bad." He himself is never late, and Lois Lamont, his secretary, says she can make appointments for him in close succession because she knows Lawrence will respect a schedule to the minute. He expects the same of others, and today he will admit readily: "If one of the boys is late a few times that worries me, because it upsets the whole band. It irritates the fellows and they get down on the late-comer. Besides, I find that lateness is a sign that a person is getting proud. He's thinking more about himself than the folks he keeps waiting."

And, further proving that he considers tardiness a character defect, Lawrence goes on to say, often in the next breath: "Good musicians alone don't make a good band. You have to have good character. I'd rather have a man with good character working for me, even if he isn't quite as good a performer. You can build up a man's musicianship if he will co-operate and work hard. It is quite often harder to change his character if it is wrong somehow."

But back in Yankton the very excusable tardiness of the boys may have been a blessing. It gave Lawrence a chance for a little reconnoitering that paid off. He tells about it this way: "I knew it would take the fellows around a half hour to get dressed and down in the dining room, so I decided that meanwhile I'd run over and see the town's new radio station."

When Lawrence reached there, he asked to speak to the "head man," and that was when he met Chandler Gurney. And who was Chandler Gurney?

Though it was much later when this personage became United States Senator from South Dakota, in Lawrence's estimation he was from the first an important figure. He possessed two valuable traits: he liked the accordion, and his family owned the radio station WNAX.

"I had a nice visit with Mr. Gurney," says Lawrence, "and at the same time I was going into a pitch about the fine troupe of musicians traveling with me."

What happened next?

It isn't hard to guess the answer. Mr. Gurney agreed to give Lawrence and his group time on an initial program of the station—beginning within the next half hour.

Lawrence eased himself from the building with as much dignity as he could, then he rounded the street corner and broke into a run. He ran all the way back to the hotel!

Bursting into the dining room without a slowdown, he yanked his friends from their seats, yelling: "We're on the air!"

Had he been yelling, "Fire!" the astonishment, and then the meek submission to his herding, could not have been more complete. The boys dropped forks full of scrambled eggs and bacon back onto their plates and went along dazedly.

"We gave our first thirty-minute broadcast entirely un-rehearsed!" he explains.

The station site was also the site of the Gurney Seed and Nursery Company. As the show progressed, the employees of the company drifted into the auditorium either one by one or in small groups, until nearly all of them were on hand to watch the orchestra that nobody had ever heard of before.

When the broadcast was over, complimentary phone calls began coming in to the station, and Mr. Gurney, taking note of them, asked Lawrence to his office for a talk.

The upshot of that talk was an offer of a week's engagement for an early morning program.

Lawrence was flabbergasted but, needless to say, managed to stammer his acceptance.

During the week the band received several bids for dance dates. These they vetoed, because with the plan to go on to New Orleans they could not tie up the future by engagements in the North. Their refusal had an effect they did not calculate: requests for their services came in with offers now of higher pay.

The rates for "name bands" of about ten pieces, at that time, ran around sixty to sixty-five dollars per night, plus a percentage of the gross receipts, so Lawrence explains: "I figured that we, with our little four-piece orchestra, would have no takers if we quoted our price at seventy-five per night, plus a whopping 70 per cent of the gross. You could have knocked us over with feathers when ballroom operators accepted our terms. This condition put us in the dance-band business in a big way."

Yes, they were in business, for with such affluence theirs for the taking they could not continue to decline dates. Furthermore, Mr. Gurney offered to extend their radio contract.

As matters finally worked out, they stayed there in Yankton for three years, and when they did go off to seek new worlds, it was only to return to Yankton, after an interval, for another three years.

Says Lawrence rather woefully: "You know, I never did get to see the Mardi Gras. I've never seen one yet, but maybe someday . . ."

Too bad that the Yankton job had to come just then?

Well, not really. Lawrence recalls: "It was in Yankton

that I met Fern," and he adds: "Yankton was a good spot for me."

Perhaps that last statement is also intended to cover the business situation, too. It would seem so from other remarks of his: "WNAX gave us plenty of radio experience. That helped a lot when I went to see Fred Miller some years later with an idea about a nationwide radio program."

WNAX Yankton likewise helped by carrying the Welk name far beyond the town's limits. Almost everywhere Lawrence went in those days, in his dance-date travels, he found that people knew him. His reputation had preceded him. Immensely gratified, he quite naturally jumped to the conclusion that he and his band must be "real wonderful."

Perhaps he was "real wonderful" but he found it rather deflating to learn a few months after he began his travels that WNAX was the sole station in existence for a radius of many, many miles, and that furthermore it was an extraordinarily powerful station. "Folks couldn't have tuned in any other station, if they had wanted to," he admits ruefully.

There could be no doubt, however, that he had improved and that he had increased his popularity. For the first time in his life he had that handy and accurate gauge of public reaction, fan mail. It didn't run to anything like his present four thousand or more letters per week, which require a battery of secretaries to process. It was something he could read personally, and he did just that, thoughtfully considering every suggestion and request, and indeed often acting upon them. For instance, when he had a complaint about his accordion playing, he took up the saxophone. It was only when other and more numerous complaints followed the change that he switched back to his first love.

However, this little excursion into a new field reinforced the notion, picked up from Kelly, that versatility within the group was highly desirable. Lawrence began urging the other men in his band to master as many instruments as possible.

Today he also likes to have his boys try out their vocal cords, and to that end he even "framed" one of them, Larry Hooper, who disclaimed "having a voice." He explains how he did it: "I just told the whole band to sing a number in chorus. Larry didn't mind joining the gang that way. What he didn't know was that I'd told the other boys to stop at the eighth bar. All of a sudden he found himself singing alone. That was what I wanted. And it sounded so good that he's been singing ever since."

If Larry isn't grateful for that ruse of Lawrence's, he should be. His very first record, "O Happy Day," has sold half a million, and he has been a popular recording star ever since.

But back to Yankton. With Operation Versatility in full swing Lawrence developed an unusual band. His men, now six in number, could play thirty-two instruments among them. They changed their name from the Lawrence Welk Novelty Band to America's Biggest Little Band.

And they had big ideas!

Lawrence signed with a booking agency and the contract stipulated that it should terminate only when the company's commission reached one million dollars.

Fabulous! But . . . oh there was a big "but," all right— the agency didn't bother to find their client bookings. Lawrence, the canny businessman, soon sized up the little game, and pointed out to the company that their inactivity had invalidated the contract.

Temporarily sans agent, Lawrence did passably well with his band until a certain fateful evening. He tells the story: "I was walking along the main street of a small South Dakota town and I happened to see through a plate-glass window that my boys were all in the poolroom. The funny part was that they were not playing pool. Instead, they were hunched over one of the green baize tables, their heads together like they were talking secrets.

"As I got closer, one of them spotted me, and quick whispered to the rest. Like a flash, they all straightened up and grabbed billiard cues.

"I didn't get it. It looked pretty queer. But I didn't have to puzzle my head too long; I soon found out what was going on."

Yes, the very next day a spokesman for the group came to Lawrence and told him. In that poolroom there had been a discussion among the members of America's Biggest Little Band, of Lawrence Welk, their leader, and they had decided that he was holding them back in their profession. His "impossible accent" and his "hick" ways were bad enough, but his playing . . . ! Crude and unrestrained, it was spoiling their chances of advancement. Why, even the owner of the radio station had joshed about putting a cushion under Lawrence's tapping foot, claiming that such exuberant timekeeping shook the whole studio. For the good of their future his musicians, to a man, were quitting.

"I felt awful about it," Lawrence admits. "Two days I was in a shock, and just about paralyzed."

But all sorts of thoughts entered his partially numbed brain. Should he go away to a new territory where he was unknown? Should he give up his idea of leading an orchestra, and join some other band?

Then through the fog of vague notions came a definite proposition. Another bandleader phoned and said: "I heard what happened, and I understand that you have bookings ahead. For myself, I haven't had much luck lately with bookings. How about your taking on my orchestra . . . you can lead it, and I'll step down and play as one of the musicians."

Ah, wasn't that a marriage made in heaven? Lawrence had the bookings and no orchestra; this man had an orchestra and no bookings.

But Lawrence didn't really want any part of it. Suddenly he knew what he *did* want.

He knew that he would prefer to hire his own orchestra, and not take on a ready-made one. Telling the other bandleader: "I'll let you know," he picked up the magazine *Billboard* and turned to the employment ads. He found that two musicians, the Reed brothers, were looking for a job. He answered that ad and thus took his first step toward building up a new orchestra.

Actually the Reeds could not join him for another two weeks; they had to give that much notice to their present employer. But now, with the spell of indecision broken, Lawrence could move ahead with his usual purposeful vigor.

Move fast he did—on the double.

Promising a steady salary instead of a percentage of the take, he hired for immediate work a drummer, a pianist, and a trumpet player and, photo-finish style, made it to his next date with a new, if incomplete, orchestra.

So it was: "Swing out, boys!"

The first notes reached his ears. Wow! Was that supposed to be music? The freshly employed trumpet player had new dentures, acquired just the day before. The teeth didn't fit, and they chattered, clack-click, clack-click, against the mouthpiece of his instrument.

"I could only pray that the audience took it for a comedy gag. The playing was something awful," Lawrence recalls. "After the first couple of numbers, I had to ask the man to stop."

The experience was an ill wind that brought the good of enlightenment. "I had a terrible band then," Lawrence concedes, "but with my old band, I had built up something. For the first time, I saw how very important a following can be. People still listened to us, just because we had a name."

Because they continued to listen, he continued to make money. In fact he made more than formerly. The steady salaries he offered may have sounded like a good proposition to the men he hired, but as it turned out, it was a better arrangement for Lawrence than his former one, whereby he had split the take evenly, with the exception of 15 per cent off the top for booking services, advertisement, transportation, and other expenses. The first week under the new setup was particularly heartening. Since he began with only an incomplete orchestra of four men, he suggested to the ballroom operators that they reduce his usual fee. However, they paid him in full. He made four hundred dollars, which was the largest weekly amount he had ever made in his lifetime—so far.

Obviously, though, people would not continue to listen indefinitely and he would not continue to make money because of a reputation gained in the past. He would have to look to the future and improve his band. Nobody realized that fact more fully than Lawrence did. He set himself to the task of procuring the finest musicians he could afford, and to working with them to bring out the best they were capable of.

"Lawrence has a marvelous knack," says his present Hollywood director, James Hobson. "He knows how to bring out the best in his men."

Call it Clue No. 13 or No. 33 if you will. At any rate, Lawrence Welk spares no pains. "Whenever I can make my band as little as 1 per cent better," he declares, "I never mind how much effort it means to do it."

Of this period of his career, while he was doing his utmost to build up the musicianship of his band, he says that the going was far from easy, but he explains: "When things are rough, that's the time when we have to work twice as hard to get over the hump."

Since he was willing to do just that, he achieved results. His engagement at the Yankton radio station was continued. Moreover, offers of dance jobs poured in as usual.

Once he and the band left the station long enough to accept a few weeks' engagement at Lake Placid, and that particular little expedition stands out in his mind more vividly than others. It was like a retreat to recoup his strength after the whirlwind existence of some years; it was like a quiet interlude graciously vouchsafed him to prepare himself for the next phase of his life.

He played there at the Bear Cub Club, and he had his days free to wander about through the shadowy stillness of the wooded mountains.

"Most of the time I used to carry my gun," he said. "Game had supplied a big part of our food back on the farm, and I've never forgotten how to hunt. But again there were times when I went out with my prayer book. I'd read a sentence or two from it, then I'd just think about God. Sometimes we have to be quiet to remember that God is with us, and will help us if we are really willing to let Him act in His own way. I think He helped me in those days. I was tired in my mind, and I was tired in my body, too, with the pace I'd been keeping. He showed me more clearly than ever what I wanted from life. It wasn't just money and success. It was something more important."

Mr. and Mrs. Ludwig Welk and their children, Mrs. Welk holding Lawrence.

Lawrence Welk and his orchestra in the late 1920's, Yankton, S.D.

The car Lawrence Welk used in the late 1920's to transport himself and his orchestra.

Fern Renner Welk in the late 1930's.

Lawrence Welk with his daughter, Donna, in 1937.

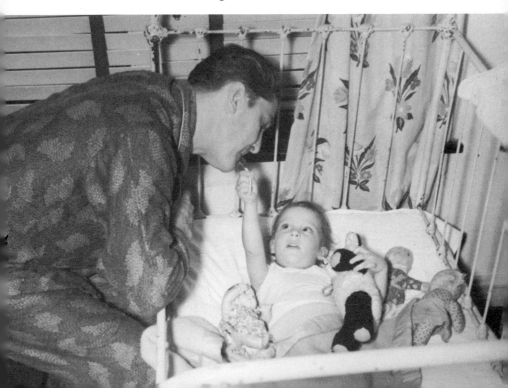

The Welk family making music at home, 1950—Lawrence, Mrs. Welk, daughters Donna and Shirley, and Lawrence, Jr.

Lawrence Welk and his Champagne Music Makers

Chapter 12

♫

"Getting to Know You"

Back to Yankton after the Lake Placid interlude, Lawrence plunged once more into hard work, and into a maze of plans for the future. The mecca of his desires was the East. At that stage of his career, he reversed Horace Greeley's advice: "Go west, young man," believing that prestige could best be won in the sophisticated East. His hope was to procure a booking there.

But plans and hard work or no, Lawrence admits: "I couldn't help noticing a bunch of good-looking student nurses from Sacred Heart Hospital, who used to come to the studio regularly."

He also mentions that he "kind of liked" the smiles and arch glances that were aimed at him through the glass partition. What's more, he didn't sprint in the opposite direction when he found that some of the girls waited for him after each broadcast, to tell him with giggles and gurgles that his playing was "perfectly marvelous," or "simply divine." He only wished that he had more time for dating.

Then on a certain memorable morning, just before going on the air, he saw *the* girl. *She* had never been there before!

As he played, his eyes kept straying toward her and lingering.

"I'd turn back to my sheet music real fast and make out like I was studying it," he says, "but a minute later there I'd be staring at her again. I couldn't help it. You know the song 'A Pretty Girl Is Like a Melody'? Well, that girl had a face like a melody."

But those quiet brown eyes of hers swept right past him to gaze abstractedly off into space. Why, she didn't seem interested even in the program!

"Soon I made no bones to it," Lawrence confesses. "I tried to get her attention by smiling at her and all. It didn't do any good. She wouldn't look my way."

The broadcast over at long last, he was on the other side of the partition in a matter of seconds. He whispered something to one of the nurses he had met before, and she introduced him to Miss Fern Renner.

He may have stuttered, he may have twisted the English words, he may have used his most guttural German accents, but he did talk to her. He even dared to ask her to dinner. He was afraid that, if he didn't make a date immediately, she might vanish into a never-never land beyond his future reach.

In response to his invitation she murmured something about being "awfully busy," so the Welk persistence came into play. Lawrence urged Miss Renner to accept, if not for tonight, then for tomorrow, and if not for tomorrow, then for the day after, but the sooner the better.

Finally she agreed to go out with him on one condition: he must include her roommate in the invitation.

"I had an answer for that," Lawrence gloats. "I told her

that I had a friend who would be happy to take out any friend of hers, and I'd arrange a foursome."

From then on Lawrence suddenly had plenty of time for dating. He would have had time whenever Fern Renner said the right word. The only trouble was that she so seldom said it.

"She kept telling me that she was tied down at the hospital. I wasn't seeing nearly enough of her." Lawrence has regrets even now.

When he was away from her, she constantly hummed in his mind like a snatch of remembered song, and as he might improvise variations of its basic theme, so he composed patterns around Fern—or, perhaps better said, little operas or dramas, à la Walter Mitty. In the libretto he, Lawrence Welk, was always the glorious hero, winning her admiration, her tender sympathy, and of course her undying love.

But the fantasy wasn't getting him anywhere. If only he could spend more time with her! Inevitably he ended on that note.

What was the trouble? Was she interested in somebody else? Or was she just being coy?

Finally he heard a rumor which really appalled him. He was told that Fern always had her nose in a medical book, and that she talked of studying medicine and becoming a doctor. Such a girl wouldn't want to become involved with a boy friend.

For days Lawrence stood dumfounded and miserable before this unexpected obstacle. How surmount that kind of thing! He could not do it by frontal attack. Perhaps a strategic approach was required. He knew that Fern worked under Dr. Abts at the hospital, and that moreover the doctor and his wife were personal friends of Fern's. She boarded in a private house next door to them and often ran in to see them and to help with their baby. Lawrence was casually acquainted with the family himself. He had consulted the doctor about a throat condition and had been told that, despite a tonsillectomy of childhood, someday there must be further surgery to remove a piece of skin which had grown back. Now Lawrence took to dropping in on the Abtses socially as well as professionally, and he asked them to put in a good word for him with "the girl next door."

"Love's Labour's Lost." Fern continued to refuse Lawrence's invitations.

Characteristically Lawrence did not admit defeat. He shifted tactics. He wasn't quite sure what he could accomplish in the long run, but at least for a time, if his new scheme worked out, he might be able to bring himself within the aura of Fern's presence.

First he made arrangements with Dr. Abts, second he procured a short leave of absence from the studio, and then he betook himself to the hospital. Marching up to the attendant at the reception desk, he politely told her that he was ready for a tonsillectomy.

The somewhat startled woman backed off from Lawrence dubiously, but when she checked with Dr. Abts, he assured her that the young man in question was a bona fide patient.

So far so good!

"The next step, I figured, was to get the hospital people to let me have Miss Renner for my nurse," Lawrence explains. "But I didn't get anywhere with that idea."

Before he could half present his plea, he was hustled

away for the preoperative ritual by another starched and efficient young lady.

Happily, however, she did serve as a willing grapevine to carry word of Lawrence's presence to Fern, who (although she was supposedly engaged in applying antiseptic bandages on another floor) managed to slip into her suitor's room after the operation to see how he was doing.

To her surprise she found that he had hemorrhaged, so, besides being feverish and half groggy from ether, he had surgical clamps in his mouth. To her further surprise, despite these oral encumberments, he managed to tell her somehow that she was "sweet." The very fact that a man in his situation would essay painful speech just to utter endearments put a slight crack in her defenses. From then on Fern discovered that there were at least a few evenings when she could leave the hospital for dates with Lawrence.

Also Fern says: "Mrs. Abts had talked to me about him. I didn't know that Lawrence himself had asked her to. Anyway, she said to me: 'I think you're being foolish not to see more of him. You couldn't find a nicer young man.'"

Actually Lawrence and Fern were well suited to one another. Whether he had the objectivity to figure that out at the time may be doubtful, but today he recognizes the fact, and he says: "We have the same religious faith, and that's real important, because it means that we think the same about big things. Both Fern and I think that making money, and all that, must not come before being good."

And besides basic belief Lawrence and Fern had other things in common. They had had similar home backgrounds; they came from the same part of the country; and (although Fern hailed from the English-speaking community of St. Anthony, North Dakota, and could handle that language with greater ease than Lawrence) they both had a German heritage.

The romance gathered momentum for a short time, then Lawrence's own profession inadvertently applied the brakes. That Eastern tour, which he had laid the groundwork for in another existence—back in the dark ages before Fern appeared—presented itself as a reality. He had no choice but to leave Fern and Yankton, at least for a short time.

Eastward ho!

Need it be said: Easterners paid no attention to Lawrence Welk—not in the year 1930? With a flat wallet he and the band hurried back to Yankton in search of another job.

"I did not want to ask Fern to be my wife until my prospects looked a little better," he explains. "I didn't think I should."

Fortunately he soon landed a six months' booking. It was at Eddie Otts' Broadmoor in Denver.

When he broke this glad news to Fern, she countered with news of her own. She announced that, when she finished her nurse's training that spring, she would be going to work in St. Paul's Hospital in Dallas, Texas. His mind did some rapid flip-flops. It was one thing for him to get back to Yankton, another to find time to go as far as Dallas. But this could not be the end of the road. He could, and did, extract a promise from Fern to write to him.

Lawrence himself had never been much for writing, but now he had an incentive. His letters must have been enough to hold Fern's interest—and maybe even to heighten it. At any rate, a few months later, when she took her vacation and went up to Yankton, she returned to Dallas by the somewhat roundabout way of Denver. As a reason she murmurs something about registering at a nurses' agency in that city, but the fact remains that the first phone call she made was not to the agency but to Lawrence.

When he heard her voice, he exclaimed: "I'll be right over," and then in his excitement he hung up without so much as a good-by.

That very evening he and Fern became engaged to be married. "I didn't want to put off asking her, now that I was doing well and saving money," he points out. "And I had some dates ahead in a couple of Tom Archer's ballrooms."

What words he used when he proposed, or if he proposed formally, he himself doesn't tell now. He can be voluble enough when he philosophizes in general about life, love, and religion, but he is completely tongue-tied about his personal romance.

No matter! He received the right answer from Fern.

But there are a few versions of the proposal built on latter-day conjecture. One version (daughter Donna's) is that Lawrence, having taken Fern up to nearby Lookout Mountain to "pop the question," gave her no real choice. "Answer 'yes' or 'no,' he said, but just let her try 'no.' He would have pushed her off the cliff."

Another version (son Larry's) is that the proposal was a mere formality. Back in the hospital in Yankton, while Lawrence lay helpless with postoperative weakness, Fern had come at him with a hypo needle, making it quite clear that "she meant business. He'd better not try to get away from her, or else . . ."

However, there is Fern's version of it. She says: "Lawrence never did propose—not really. I was wearing a ring, and he took one look at it and blurted out: 'Oh, where did you get that? I was going to ask you myself!'

"When I explained that it didn't mean what he thought, he asked if I smoked or drank. When I said no, he began to talk about us getting married, as though it were all settled."

But why had Fern been so cool to him in the beginning? Had she really planned to be a doctor?

"It's true," she says. "I was very serious about my work. I stayed longer in operating-room assistance than other nurses. I had a vague notion I'd like to be a surgeon. Mostly, though, I was afraid of a musician. I figured that musicians, like sailors, would have a girl in every port. Then, too, I thought that a bandleader would have to be conceited."

She goes on to recall the girls in the hospital, who acted "so silly." She didn't want to be just another of Lawrence's F.F.F.s, his Fluttering Female Fans. In the end, however, she couldn't resist him and words on Lookout Mountain were superfluous. She had already capitulated.

But what made her capitulate? She gives her reasons: "Well, you look at Lawrence, and see he was—he is, a very handsome man . . . that smile of his . . . and . . . and everything about him. And I could notice so many wonderful qualities in him. He talked so beautifully about his mother, not only lovingly, but you might say respectfully and even reverently. Then, much as he wanted success in his career, he didn't talk like a man who would do anything low or mean to get it. He'd mention the law of God, or the will of God. A man who tries to live by that can't go very far wrong, can he?"

And, to prove that her evaluation of him was correct, she cites an incident which occurred in their early married life. Lawrence could see the possibility of a booking which augured everything he was striving for—additional money, prestige, and a boost upward toward the ultimate goal. He let it be known through his agents that he was available for the opening, and the hint came back that the plum would soon be his for the picking. He was so excited and happy that he talked of nothing else for days.

Then suddenly he was silent. He seemed moody, out of sorts, and quite unlike himself. Several times Fern woke in the middle of the night to find him tossing sleepless at her side. She couldn't imagine what had come over him, and she was still trying to figure out some tactful way of asking him when he confided in her.

He had refused the much-coveted booking, and now he saw nothing in sight. His refusal to take the next giant step upward, he said, had cut him off from the future—from a whole series of possible steps later. He felt as though he was trapped in a dark blind alley.

But why had he refused the billet he wanted so dearly? There was reason enough! The key person involved in the booking had turned out to be a woman who had met Lawrence a few times and had apparently been attracted to him. She had made it quite clear that for the "favor" of hiring the band she expected in return a little amorous attention from Lawrence. Conscience dictated his course.

Fern has never regretted the evening on Lookout Mountain or her subsequent marriage to Lawrence. Far from it! She is apparently so content with her lot that on one occasion a friend could not resist challenging: "You can't really believe that Lawrence is perfect. You must be like the rest of us—we wives usually have a few stray complaints. Aren't there some things about him that get you down?"

Fern thought a minute before she answered: "There's one quirk of his. He will forget and wipe his razor on my good towels. He knows I hate that, and like a little boy who's been naughty, he will hang the towel backward so that I don't see the spot that the razor's made."

If that's all a wife can dredge up by way of complaint, it is a pretty good testimonial of a happy marriage.

But what about that marriage? And the wedding—the when, where, and how of it?

♫

Chapter 13

"We'll Stroll the Lanes Together"

It was settled. They were to be married. They had only to name the date. But meantime Fern went back to Dallas and her job there. Via the mails they made their plans.

Lawrence urged a mid-April wedding, as that would allow them to go to Niagara Falls for a honeymoon, en route to Albany, where a late-April engagement was booked for him at the De Witt Clinton Hotel. April 18 (1931) was the date finally agreed upon.

Neither of their families would be able to attend. Indeed Lawrence figured that the only people likely to show up would be Dr. and Mrs. Abts and the boys of the little band. For that reason, as well as to hang onto the few dollars they had saved, Lawrence and Fern decided to make the wedding as quiet and simple as possible.

"Frills aren't important anyway," avers Lawrence. "Fern and I just wanted to do it right—in church with God's blessing."

On the date set Lawrence would be playing at Tom Archer's Rigadoon ballrooms in Sioux City, so they chose the Cathedral of the Epiphany of that town for the place of the wedding. For the time they selected the unusual hour of 5:30 A.M.—but with reasons galore. It would mean only a brief interval between the time that Lawrence would finish playing for a dance and the ceremony at day-break Mass; it was shortly after Fern's train from Dallas would be arriving in town; and, lastly, it would allow them to squeeze in a wedding breakfast for their friends and still get an early start on a trip eastward, which they had to begin by midmorning in order to make Lawrence's next scheduled engagement.

Now at any wedding a nervous groom is standard equipment, but at this wedding the priest who witnessed the Sacrament, Father Leo McCoy, was also nervous. He was a young fellow, fresh from the seminary, serving his initial assignment as curate, and this was his first Nuptial Mass. He went through it painstakingly, then, heaving a sigh of relief, dismissed the couple. However, just as they were leaving the church, he emitted a panicky little gasp and called them back with the cryptic exclamation: "Something's wrong!"

Lawrence says: "I know my heart came to a full stop before Father managed to get out the words explaining what it was about. He had forgotten to bless the ring—and that's all."

More comic relief was in store for the young benedict. Accompanied only by Dr. and Mrs. Abts (who appropriately enough "stood up" for the pair, whose romance they had aided and abetted), he and Fern made a fresh try at leaving the church. They did actually pass through the doors this time but were immediately arrested by a strange sight. There, sitting on the cathedral steps, was a huddled mass, composed of the boys of the band, each clutching in his fist a bag of rice to throw at the newlyweds, but each, believe it or not, sound asleep.

Evidently 5:30 of a raw spring morning is too much for even the best of friends!

Laughing foolishly and excitedly, they headed for the Martin Hotel and breakfast. The group broke up in time, but just barely, Lawrence calculated, to go by their respective rooms, pick up their luggage, and get a reasonably early start on the Eastern trip. Lawrence assembled his own and Fern's bags, stowed them in the trunk compartment of the car, and went back to his room for his accordion. All set?

Lawrence took a quick look around to see if he had forgotten anything, and in that split second the phone rang.

"Hello," he said into the mouthpiece, then "What?" and more sharply "What's that again?"

Fern, standing by his side, sensed trouble, and when Lawrence gave her a weak little smile intended to be reassuring, it only confirmed her suspicions of impending difficulty.

Finally he hung up and, no other course being open, broke the news: the Albany engagement had been canceled. He and the band were without a job. What's more, nothing was in sight but a few one-night stands in Wisconsin.

Lawrence thought of Tom Archer, for whom the band had just played. Tom owned ballrooms in Sioux City, Sioux Falls, Des Moines, and in St. Joseph, Missouri, and Omaha, Nebraska. This man liked Lawrence's music, and, says the bandleader: "Tom was a real friend. After every job I did for him we'd sit down together and talk over my playing, trying to figure out if we could make anything better. He really wanted to do the best for the folks out front, just like I did. I thought such a lot of his ideas that

I once offered him a percentage of our take to give us advice, but he said that he wasn't sure his ideas were that good. He'd tell us anything he knew without money. He was strong for earning every cent he got. I admired him a lot."

Despite this fine association, and despite the fact that in later years Lawrence was to play the Archer circuit again many times, in April 1931 Tom had to confess that he had no openings at the moment. According to Lawrence's bookers, other ballroom operators had the same tale.

Up till this point Lawrence had been doing well. "It took marriage and me to have the Depression catch up with him," says Fern, who can afford to be facetious about it now.

It was the few one-nighters, and then a long blank stretched ahead.

Arriving for the first date in La Crosse, Lawrence made the sort of slip that people joke about but never believe actually happens: he signed the hotel register Lawrence Welk and Fern Renner. He was about to walk away serenely unaware of his mistake when he caught the expression on the clerk's face. He could only scratch out the second name and preface his own with Mr. and Mrs.

Poor Fern! She saw it all, including the clerk's wink as he handed Lawrence the key, and she comments: "I was a complete hermit the twenty-four hours we were in that hotel. I didn't dare stick my nose outside the door of my room. I was too embarrassed."

After the few one-nighters were filled, the question of lining up more jobs became urgent. To expedite matters, Lawrence proposed that they go to Chicago, for he reasoned that a big bustling place would logically offer many possibilities. So it was off to the windy city for the little group. While there, they lived in an obscure hotel on Wabash Avenue, with rates of a dollar to a dollar and a half per room. From that anchorage Lawrence made daily excursions to his booker's office with Mr. Micawber's hope that something would "turn up."

"It was a funny honeymoon," by Lawrence's admission. "I was in a kind of panic, wondering and worrying what to do next. And every day our little roll of money got smaller and smaller. But Fern and I did have real wonderful moments anyhow. We'd slip away from the boys, and hand by hand we'd walk along the Lake Shore Drive to watch the sun on the water. You know, it reminded us of the smile of heaven beaming down on us, and we kept telling each other that everything was going to be fine."

Once during the Chicago sojourn they made a day's trip to Decatur, where Lawrence's old friend, Max Fichtner, and his family then lived. The expedition was "real nice in lots of ways," but Lawrence emphasizes: "They asked us to dinner. We had sauerbraten and dumplings."

Evidently, to two hungry young people who had been living on beans and coffee bought in a cheap diner, a home-cooked meal was nothing short of nectar and ambrosia.

But one good dinner didn't help them solve that nagging question of how to find a job. Lawrence's money approached the vanishing point. In the beginning he had paid not only his own and Fern's expenses but those of the boys as well. When the day came that that was no longer possible, the boys attempted to fend for themselves. Before Lawrence's eyes the band bit by bit disintegrated.

"It got so that I couldn't even buy food for Fern and me," he recalls.

"Before we were married, Fern told me that she couldn't cook. I laughed that away, saying: 'Then we'll eat in restaurants,' and I meant it. Now I couldn't buy restaurant meals, or even food to cook. A little bread and cheese and stuff like that kept us going, but most of the time we were close to hungry. I tried not to let Fern see how awful scared I got. I couldn't sleep at night worrying about what to do. Finally, I figured that, whatever happened, we couldn't stay where we were. There just had to be a job somewhere, and if my bookers couldn't find it, then it was up to me to go from place to place looking for one myself."

And he reasoned that the Dakotas, where he was known, might after all prove the best hunting ground for jobs, and for finding musicians to replace those who had left him.

It was time for him to remember his own favorite dictum about "hard conditions" and making an extra effort "to get over the hump."

Lawrence literally worked their way home, bartering music-making for a night's lodging or a day's food. Once there, with faith, courage, and hope to bolster them, they managed to dig up enough jobs to scrimp along in the manner they were accustomed, lo these many weeks.

While Lawrence was in that part of the country, he had an opportunity to take Fern for a short visit to the farm to meet Mamma and Papa. It was a warm and jolly reunion and certainly a contrast to the harried and hungry existence the newlyweds had so far had together. Sisters and brothers kept stopping in with new babies to show off so that laughter, singing and backslapping made the old Welk home echo and re-echo with sounds of merriment.

When Lawrence left with Fern, it was to accept a summer-long job at Twin Lakes, Wisconsin, which his bookers had landed for him. Things were looking up—at least to a degree. He had a semi-permanent job.

In those Depression years music jobs, permanent or otherwise, were growing scarcer by the minute. On all sides of him Lawrence could see his confreres abandoning the profession, to seek work which might bring them a steadier income.

For some months, anyhow, Lawrence's new job would ensure meals for all of them and there would be a little cash to boot. The compensation offered was room and board for the band, plus $300 a month. If the booking agent's fee took $60 and Union dues $20, $220 still was left to split among the eight of them and, says Lawrence: "It was something."

The troupe left the Dakotas for Wisconsin in good spirits to see what lay ahead.

♫

Chapter 14

"There's a Long, Long Trail"

On Inauguration Day, when some Washington hotels were asking forty dollars per diem for a room ordinarily billed at fifteen, Lawrence remarked: "Many a time I've had a room for thirty-five or fifty cents a night. Some of them weren't so fancy of course, but I guess the worst we ever had was the room at Twin Lakes."

The troupe arrived by car and the ballroom manager, having introduced himself, took the travelers to their living quarters. He led them around to the rear of the dance hall to what looked like a lean-to, adjacent to the large structure. Here was the band's hide-out—one small cubicle, its four walls each lined with beds.

"But I have a private room for you and the missus," the manager informed Lawrence, and entered the ballroom.

Lawrence and Fern followed in his footsteps and gaped over his shoulder as he threw open the door of an erstwhile storage closet, "furnished." The furniture, wedged into the cramped space, consisted of a sagging bed (on which hung dejectedly a plaid blanket, heavy with the grime of years) and a couple of tired, rickety chairs—period. No curtains graced the tiny window; instead it was criss-crossed with cobwebs. No paint covered the walls; they were decorated only by a few rusty nails (intended to hold clothes) protruding from the bare boards.

But the manager was talking. He was explaining that there was indoor plumbing—see the "MEN" and "WOMEN" signs in the ballroom? As for bathing—well of course the lake would serve.

"I was used to roughing it," says Lawrence, "so I didn't think much about this till I took a look at Fern's face. She seemed awful sad. I reached out to pat her hand and tell her it wouldn't be too bad, and right off she burst into tears."

For three days those tears flowed. Such an abundance of salt water should have washed the place out, but dirt is stubborn stuff. It didn't budge until, on the fourth day, Fern dried her eyes, rolled up her sleeves, and set to scrubbing with all the vigor that hospital training had taught her.

"My wife is the cleanest person and the most particular housekeeper in the world," Lawrence asserts. "Now as I look back, I don't see how I ever had the nerve to take her into a place like that."

Nonetheless she grew to like it. She bought paint for the walls, a ruffled organdy curtain for the window, a bright flowered spread for the bed, and by sheer feminine magic turned the drab "room" into a gay and cozy nook.

It is understandable why Shirley (now Mrs. Robert Fredericks) says of her mother: "She's a genius with a home. Now that I'm married, I'm always trying to do things the way Mother did them. I can't understand some of my friends—the girls I graduated from college with: they duck work around the home for an office job where they must take somebody else's dictation and pound away at a mechanical typewriter. But housework is so creative. The less you have to go on financially, the more of a challenge it is. Then it's so satisfying to make somebody as contented and comfortable as Mother has always made Daddy, despite some of their fly-by-night diggings."

He was comfortable and contented there at Twin Lakes —and he was happy. The summer danced blithely along and was crowned at the end with news of something Lawrence called "a blessed condition." Fern discovered that she was going to have a baby.

Good news followed good news. Another booking was ready for the Lawrence Welk band at the Mirador Ballroom in Phoenix, Arizona, at $425 a week.

With the few dollars saved from the pittance received at Twin Lakes they could buy gas to get there—and not much more. But that was good enough. They set off.

"During the hot days of an October Indian summer," Lawrence recalls, "we headed southward across the desert in three old jalopies. The trip would not have been a rose bed anyhow, but with Fern pregnant, and in a car like ours that broke down ever so often, it was worse. Then, of all things, Fern kept craving pickles."

Along the sparsely settled routes that they followed no pickle vendors appeared. Finally, in a little town where they stopped for gas, Lawrence spotted a grocery store. He counted his small horde of money, took out a whole dollar and slipped away, to return a few minutes later with a huge two-quart jar in a brown paper bag. Bearing it proudly to his ladylove, he asked in a voice that he tried to keep casual: "How about a pickle?"

To his surprise and chagrin she answered just as casually: "Oh, don't bother to buy any now. I did have the worst hankering for them a while back, but now I don't care if I ever see one. In fact they'd probably make me sick the way I feel at this point."

When the exchequer is as low as Lawrence's was just then, you don't throw away food for which you've paid good money. You eat it. Lawrence subsisted on a pickle diet for the rest of the trip. Need anybody ask why he doesn't like pickles today?

Arriving in Phoenix, they followed written directions about locating the Mirador.

"We found it, all right," Lawrence says, "but what a shock it gave us. The windows were shuttered, and the doors boarded over. We didn't know what to make of it."

A few inquiries ferreted out the facts: the place had been closed for lack of business. So-o! There they were stranded in a place where they didn't know a soul, and with no job or money in sight.

This was worse than Chicago! There wasn't enough money between them for the cheapest of hotel accommodations or for enough food to carry them through the next twenty-four hours.

Lawrence took stock of the situation and went into action.

He had one possession worth a little cash. It was the diamond ring he had bought at the first flush of prosperity with Peerless Entertainers.

"I never thought I'd part with it deliberately," he said in relating this incident, and then he told about the time he had nearly lost it accidentally. While he was swimming at Twin Lakes, the ring had slipped from his finger and, declares Lawrence: "I figured that meant good-by. I felt awful, but this is like a believe-it-or-not Ripley tale. When

I was diving into the clear water, I actually found it. Of all places it had dropped around a reed, growing on the lake's mud bottom.

"I'd worn it like a sign of my first success and it reminded me to keep trying to go ahead. I went over all that in my mind as I took the ring down to a pawnbroker in Phoenix. He gave me seventy-five dollars for it."

Now they could eat! But Lawrence knew he would have to take further steps if they wanted to go on eating for long. Working with electric energy, he managed to round up all of the twenty-two stockholders of the ballroom, and, addressing them in his thick German accent, he pleaded for a reopening of the place. Their set faces indicated that his argument so far was not convincing them, so he played his trump card: he promised that if the venture should be a financial loss he would shoulder the debt.

That week the ballroom opened.

In the course of the following weeks Lawrence and the boys drew good crowds night after night. "It seemed no time at all," Lawrence exulted, "before I had the money to get back my ring."

Today TV audiences can see that ring on the fourth finger of his left hand. If this talisman determines in any way the kind of forging ahead Lawrence has done, then the pawnbroker who allowed seventy-five dollars for it grossly underrated its value.

Of course the Depression still dragged on for a few more years, which meant that there were more bad stretches ahead. "But," says Fern, "after Phoenix, I never worried. When I saw how Lawrence managed there against those odds, I just knew he'd always find a way to get along, no matter what."

Well, ups and downs are to be expected in show business. They are as much a part of it as the moves Lawrence speaks of "from pillars to posts." In the next months the little orchestra traveled in Texas, Arizona, Oklahoma, and Kansas, Fern along with them. But in the spring she let them go to a Denver engagement without her. She wanted to stay in Dallas until the baby was born, so that she could receive the care of Dr. McLeod, whom she had known, worked with and admired at St. Paul's Hospital.

Lawrence parted with her reluctantly.

♫

Chapter 15

"Rock-a-bye Baby"

It was a girl!

On April 29, Shirley Jean arrived while her father was off to the North, in Denver.

"Way early in the morning, a nurse friend of Fern's put in a call from Dallas with the news," Lawrence recounts, "and my landlady, who answered the phone, has probably been talking about it ever since."

Sleepily the good woman padded downstairs in slippers and robe when the phone rang but, going up again to summon her boarder, she was fully awake and curious. Not many expensive long-distance calls came to her house of a predawn. It must mean that Mr. Welk's wife had the baby.

She rapped on his door. To her surprise there was no response. "He's sure a heavy sleeper," she muttered.

But in a case like this, she decided, it was right and proper for her just to "bust in" and wake the man up. She tried the door. It wasn't locked. Opening it, she began: "Mr. Welk . . ." and then broke off.

She saw that the bed had not been slept in! She glanced around as though she half expected Lawrence might be crouching behind the bureau, or in a closet, or on the little porch which opened off his room.

"What'll I tell 'em? It don't look good at this hour, but I'll have to tell 'em, he ain't in," the woman murmured to herself.

Afterward, when she had delivered her message and received the news from the other end, she went back to the scene of the mystery, to try to figure out Lawrence's disappearance act.

It didn't take long. Although the bed remained empty, and the room unoccupied, she noticed something on the porch which had escaped her attention before. It was a dark object protruding from the snowdrift in the corner under the eaves. It looked like a foot, clad in an Argyle sock.

Sure enough, that's what it was! Mr. Welk must be under that snow.

By this time her bustling about had had an effect. The snowdrift began to quiver, and a tousled head erupted at the far end of it. A moment later, shaking himself like a dog emerging from a bath, Lawrence stood up.

"What on earth?" exclaimed the woman. Maybe all musicians were crazy, but she didn't figure that any were this bad!

"I tried to explain to her that I had grown up on a farm. I liked fresh air. I liked to sleep outdoors. And I told her I hadn't any idea there'd be a snowstorm during the night. After all it was April," Lawrence points out.

And then it was his turn to ask questions. The lady wouldn't be waking him up at this hour unless . . .

She lost no time in confirming his surmise: he was a father—of a baby girl, weighing five pounds, twelve ounces. Then without more ado she turned on her heel and left, presumably to try for a few more winks before the alarm clock proclaimed the start of another workday.

"I just stood there, staring after her for a couple of minutes. Then I made a dash down the stairs to the phone in the lower hall. I had to put in a call to Dallas."

Connected at last with the maternity floor of the hospital, Lawrence was answered by a crisp, impersonal voice. Despite the lump in his throat he managed to ask quaveringly for the nurse friend who had phoned him earlier. When he had her on the line, he blurted out the dread question, "What chance has she? Will the baby live?"

"Why, Lawrence," came the calm reply, "what's the matter? Our bulletins show that both mother and baby are doing nicely. And I've talked to Fern myself, and—"

"But she's so tiny!" stammered Lawrence.

"Babies usually come in wee sizes," his friend assured him.

"But . . . but only twelve ounces!"

"What did you say?" the nurse shot back.

"Twelve ounces," Lawrence repeated.

Over the wire came something suspiciously like a giggle, then the nurse explained to Lawrence that his baby weighed five pounds, twelve ounces, and that he had nothing to fear about her size. It was quite normal.

He hung up the phone and stumbled upstairs, his face bearing a dazed expression.

"Was I glad when Fern and Shirley got to Denver, and I could see for myself that they were OK," he says. "Seeing makes believing."

But he had to wait six weeks for that day. Meantime he improved his shining hours by writing a song in honor of his daughter which he entitled "You're My Home Sweet Home."

He was not able to place it with any song editor, so he decided to publish it privately. The venture cost him four hundred dollars, and that was four hundred dollars too much, for the song brought him no returns.

This is not a reflection on the little daughter, who Lawrence declares solemnly "was beautiful." He also declares that she was frightening, and he recalls: "Fern laughed at me because I was afraid to hold my own baby. And I was afraid of her in other ways, too. I'd look at her, and all of a sudden it would hit me again that I was her father. It was up to me—to Fern and me—to teach her to follow God's laws, so that she would have a chance at the right kind of life. That's the big job of parents."

Perhaps it was these musings which drew Lawrence's mind more often than ever to his own parents and made him decide to take his daughter home to the farm to show her off to the folks.

"Of course, I often went back to the farm anyhow," he says. "I'd run home whenever I was in the Dakotas and had a free interval. I kept that up real regular, till my mother died."

His mother's death occurred in 1940, and to this day Lawrence regrets that he could not be with her in her last hours.

"I knew she had been ill for a long time with diabetes, but I didn't know she was really low until about twenty-four hours before she died. I was in Pittsburgh when this wire came, and I rushed out to the airport, but all the planes were grounded because of a heavy fog. For a long,

long time I felt awful that I wasn't there to say good-by to Mother."

Lawrence was, however, present when his father died, a few years before that, though he was almost killed getting there.

Again the weather had been treacherous and Lawrence drove over icy roads from Minneapolis to Strasburg. Just before he reached his destination he had an accident. "It happened so quickly that I hardly know what happened. I put on the brakes, I think. Anyway the car skidded, spun around, and turned over in a ditch. I crawled out kind of shaken up, bruised and cut, but I was a lot more scared than hurt."

Of course Ludwig died completely reconciled to his son's career. In fact Lawrence recalls that after the first few visits made within a year or so of his leaving the farm his father's misgivings vanished as completely as the echo of yesterday's discord. From then on old Ludwig never missed an opportunity to point out to his neighbors: "My son, Lawrence, the bandleader, you know . . ."

And by the time that Lawrence and Fern arrived with the new baby, Ludwig was prouder than ever. He opened up the schnapps and invited his friends over.

Drink to Lawrence Welk, everybody! *Prosit!*

But this visit soon came to an end with another engagement looming up.

On the road again?

Lawrence and Fern looked at each other questioningly. Shirley Jean would change their life. They realized it suddenly. Fern could not traipse all over the map with a new baby. Besides the baby's health might suffer if she were constantly on the move.

A competent nurse—was that the answer? Somebody to take full-time care of Shirley and leave Fern free to travel? If Lawrence and Fern thought of such an idea, they quickly discarded it. To them that expedient meant ducking responsibility.

"We could see only one thing to do," says Lawrence, "find some sort of permanent place for Fern and the baby to stay, while I'd go off to my engagements, leaving them behind."

But neither Fern nor Lawrence liked being separated.

Finally Fern came up with an idea: "Lawrence, couldn't you find some work besides music? There must be lots of things you could do that would keep you in one place. How about it? Then we could have a real home—be together all the time."

Lawrence turned the thought over and over in his mind. Should he act on it? And if so how? They were not easy questions for him to answer. "It got so I was real disturbed," he admits. "Seems like I didn't have much peace in my mind. I knew for sure from home training that real peace can come only by doing right, but I was having a hard time trying to figure just what was right."

On the one hand, Lawrence saw in the recesses of his mind a dream kept warmly aglow by the fires of his imagination: it was the dream of playing in big cities like New York and Chicago, and making many thousands of people happy with music. He believed in that dream. Someday he felt it could be reality—provided he pursued his music steadfastly. At times that pursuit seemed a duty.

At other times came doubt. He was a husband and father, so he should step off this musical merry-go-round and settle down in a real home.

"I couldn't decide, even though I prayed about it," Lawrence says. "Finally I figured I wouldn't go wrong by trying out another business, because that was probably the more generous way. And I told the good Lord I'd do the best I could with it, and leave results to Him."

That meant Lawrence would curtail his musical activities and cut down on traveling. It meant that he would forget the vision of New York and Chicago. "By the time Shirley would be old enough to go to school I planned to be done with tours," Lawrence says, "and music itself would be mostly a side line. I didn't know what other business I'd try. I didn't think that made much difference."

Meanwhile he had engagements, previously lined up, which took him to Texas.

♫

Chapter 16

"Deep in the Heart of Texas"

In Dallas, Lawrence came upon a hotel, flaunting a "FOR SALE" sign. He went inside and examined the place. What he saw in a first hasty look pleased him. On the top floor there was a five-room suite, intended for family living. "It's just right for us," Lawrence concluded in a matter of minutes.

Then he began to calculate: profits from the rest of the building would supply him with a handsome, even luxurious livelihood. The sale price, Depression-influenced, was to his mind ridiculously low: it might even justify the otherwise-questionable expedient of borrowing money. But enough said.

Impulsively Lawrence did borrow the down payment, and in very short order became the proprietor of a hotel. He changed its name from the Main Peak to the Lawrence and went off to tell Fern the news.

"That husband of mine used to have a visionary streak," she says. "It's funny, too, because instinctively he was—and is—cautious for the most part. But when we were first married, he'd have those unexpected flights every once in a while."

Apparently there were times when the practical Fern

had to pull the more romantic Lawrence down to earth and comb the stardust from his hair.

Be that as it may, in 1932 Lawrence found himself in the hotel business, about which he knew nothing.

He moved in with his family, and was confidently striding through the lobby on the first day of his proprietorship, when one of the guests ran up to him, grabbed his arm, and gasped breathlessly: "If you're the owner of this hotel, come quickly. Something awful has happened. I know it has."

With that the fellow bolted down the hall, and at his heels followed Lawrence, throwing out, staccato-style: "What . . . ? What is it . . . ?"

"Come on," the guest flung back over his shoulder as he ran. "Can't you smell the gas? She may have left the gas logs on." He slid to a stop. "This is it. This is her room, and she's been very despondent lately, talking about . . ."

Lawrence needed no further explanation. He could smell the gas all right. Instantly (though he had in those days no TV who-dun-its to teach him the technique) he lunged forward against the door, using all the strength he could summon. It gave way, allowing him to stagger into the room. On the floor lay a body—that of a woman.

"I clamped one hand on my nose, and with the other hand I dragged her from the room. Then I ran to call the police," he recalls. "They came right away, and was I relieved that they brought the woman round to consciousness."

So the Lawrence Hotel venture began with an attempted suicide!

It continued with other melodramatic episodes, though Lawrence himself was not on hand for the next one. When he bought the place, he had a number of musical commitments ahead, and he explains: "I had to take care of those. That's why I had to leave Fern in charge of the hotel for a little while."

The day after Lawrence set out for an across-state job, she awoke to make an appalling discovery: she found that a bootlegger was operating a full-fledged business from one of the hotel rooms.

"I sold the place only five months after I'd bought it," Lawrence says with a wry grin.

However, he managed a small profit, so monetarily the enterprise wasn't too bad. Lawrence has never been a slouch as a businessman, but admittedly he has used his commercial talents to best advantage in the "music business."

In the years that followed, without neglecting the band, he periodically tried further side-line ventures. He bought and managed an electrical store in Yankton, South Dakota; he took up chicken farming in Omaha, Nebraska; he opened a restaurant in Mason City, Iowa; and he distributed chewing gum throughout the Midwest.

None of these ventures was really successful, but that was not their outstanding drawback. Fern realized the trouble long before Lawrence had run this gamut. In fact, while they were still at the Texas hotel, she admitted: "Lawrence can't be himself apart from music. He lives in a state of suspended animation till he can get back to playing again."

Very early, then, though her husband kept on trying out further enterprises, Fern deciphered the mural handwriting, and she declares: "I made up my mind I might just as well accept my role as the wife of a bandleader, objectionable features and all."

Although by far the worst feature was the separation, from Fern's viewpoint there were others, too. Back in her student days at Yankton she had found out about the oh-so-coy F.F.F.s, the Fluttering Female Fans. Now she saw that certain of their more brazen sisters pursued the bandleader openly. True, Lawrence was adroit in dodging these "ladies"; on the other hand, he considered it part of his job as entertainer to dance with his circumspect patrons, and who could tell if a few of these might not turn out to be troublemakers?

"If I hadn't known for sure that Lawrence really stuck by his principles, this phase of his profession would have given me some sleepless nights," Fern confesses.

Nor did the musical highroad prove the royal road to fame and fortune, in the 1930's. It seemed to Fern that selling apples on a street corner would have been almost as lucrative as music.

For a while the band had an assignment which offered limited salary and room and board. (The job was to play dinner music in several of the Hilton hotels, in Lubbock, Big Spring, Abilene, etc., and Lawrence gladly took it, explaining to his wife: "We get good living for our work, and our hours leave us plenty of time later in the evening to earn money at ballrooms.")

Then Fern was plagued by another worry—temporary to be sure, but still a worry. In those days many of the oil towns of west Texas to which Lawrence traveled were not quiet little hamlets. Her recurring nightmare had to do with her innocent husband somehow becoming involved in the shootings and brawls which by some accounts were as common as cactus.

Lawrence himself used to tell tales of the time he dipped briefly into Texas with the Peerless Entertainers. "It was a regular thing at rehearsals," he said, "to have one of the boys suddenly give a mighty whack on the drum, imitating a pistol shot. That was a signal. We were supposed to do a practice dive behind the upright piano."

Could reminiscence have embroidered the stories? Fern would shudder when she thought of them, and she would wish that her Lawrence could steer clear of every dance hall or night club in the Southwest's frontier land.

Nor can there be any doubt that he saw more than enough to goggle the eyes—or even turn the stomach of—a boy who had scarcely hobnobbed with anybody but sober-living farmers. Some of the itinerant musicians (coming from all parts of the country) smoked marijuana, and were given to immoral high-jinks of all varieties. "But," points out Lawrence, "they were not my boys. My boys behaved very well, fortunately."

A present-day friend of Lawrence's says that the band-leader confided to him: "The most terrible temptations I ever had in my life were those that plagued me as a real young man in Texas. But when I left there, and could still look at myself straight and unashamed, I knew one thing for sure: we get the strength to do right just as long as we really and truly want to do right."

If Lawrence had been another kind of man, a creature more prone to stray from the strait and narrow, his choice of music *versus* commercial business might have been different. At any rate, Fern might likely have summoned up what womany wiles she could, in an effort to make it different.

As it was, she encouraged him to stay with music. But despite this Lawrence had to make up his own mind. He was slow about it. Or perhaps in a sense he never really reached a clear-cut decision at all. For a short period only he tried to curtail traveling, and intermittently for a long period he tried to juggle a side-line business, which, so he kidded himself, he might eventually, upon leaving the music business, make his main interest. But throughout he never ceased for a moment to work for and with the band.

In fact, while the Welks were still in Texas, Lawrence added something new—and something very important—to the band.

♫

Chapter 17

"Boys and Girls Together"

"It happened almost accidentally," says Lawrence. "One evening, Fern and I were dressing to go to dinner at the cafeteria where we played, and the radio was on. We heard this girl singing over station WFAA. She sounded real wonderful, and all of a sudden Fern asked: 'Why don't you have a girl singer?' I figured she was right. A girl singer would help the band."

Now at the time Lawrence was supposedly curtailing his musical activities, but whenever he thinks of anything that may help the band, he can no more resist going after it than a dog can resist a proffered bone.

On this occasion he lost no time either. Since both WFAA and the cafeteria were located in the Baker Hotel, Fern and Lawrence stopped by the station on their way to dinner and invited the girl—Maxine Gray was her name —to share their meal. Before they had finished eating, Lawrence had persuaded her to take the job he offered.

Maxine was followed through the years by a parade of girl singers, most of whom Lawrence avows were also "real wonderful." The description includes a great deal, for in a moralizing tone he adds the explanation that his ideal of a good girl singer is the adroit miss who knows how to be a "sweetheart to all, but a sweetheart to none."

Although Lawrence can wax quite eloquent on the virtues of his "little girls," he can be just as voluble about the problems that some of them cause. Surprisingly he gives top billing among problems to the Managing Mammas of the girls. In the capacity of chaperons they often travel with their daughters, and does that complicate matters! Says Lawrence aggrievedly: "There was one lady, a real long time ago, who told Fern to stay home, that there wasn't room for her to travel in the car with us. And I've had them tell me what numbers their daughters should sing, or complain to me because their daughters didn't get a large enough share of the spotlight."

One time when the band was playing in New York, also some years ago, Lawrence invited his Champagne Lady and her mother to dinner to discuss some difficulties, but the latter's pride resented the least suggestion or criticism of her dear child. After an hour or so of haranguing Lawrence, telling him how wrong he was, and how right her daughter was, she ended up demanding: "Outside my daughter, what's there to your band? Without her, you wouldn't have a band at all."

"OK, lady," Lawrence replied. "We'll see if you're right. Take your daughter and go back home on the first train running."

That was the knockout. The lady had no return punch. She could only gasp.

But Lawrence worries about a mother not only because her vanity is so often, as he says, "a thorn in my ribs," but for "real serious reasons." Usually the dowager plays lady-in-waiting to the shining star of the family, not so much because of mother love, but rather because she relishes the ego-building effect of the job. To keep it, she will flee husband and other children, plus the home fires she should be tending.

"I don't like it," Lawrence says. "That kind of pride can lead to disaster. I remember a case where it caused a divorce for one of these mothers."

Also, he explains, it can cause gross selfishness toward the "favored" child. The mother will block her daughter's future happiness in order to bask longer in the reflected glow of the spotlight.

Lawrence recounts: "I used to tease one of my singers sometimes about her boy friends, but if the mother heard me, she'd get real mad, and say: 'Oh, Lawrence, cut that out. My daughter isn't ready to think of love.'"

Nor does employing married girls, though it may push Friend Mamma into the background, eliminate difficulties. "A married girl singer can put an awful strain on her home life, if she doesn't watch her step," declares Lawrence.

But be it said: all Lawrence's problems do not revolve around his girl singers. Lawrence will admit, if a bit ruefully: "The boys get proud too."

Pride Lawrence defines as "a kind of dishonesty which makes people blind to what's what," and he says, "To keep going ahead, a person has to see facts, and that means the faults which creep in, as well as the good points. Only the person who sees facts can know what to correct."

Any other problems?

"Jealousy can be real bad," Lawrence confesses, "and it has given me troubles with the band in the past. But I'm glad to say there isn't much of it among my boys today."

That last statement is backed up by Bill Lennon (father

of the winsome Lennon Sisters). He cannot make enough complimentary comments about the *esprit de corps* which animates all the band members, making them work together for the good of the whole, without personal bickering or jealousy. "You know," he points out, "those fellows could have resented my little girls being brought in from the outside. Instead every last one of the boys has gone out of his way to show my youngsters kindness and consideration. Part of the credit goes to Lawrence. People just can't seem to be petty around him."

Undoubtedly Lawrence would say that the credit goes in large part to those girls—"the loveliest children on television."

Next to jealousy comes Troublemaker No. 3, drink. "In the old days, that used to be worse," says Lawrence, and he tells about a former band member, "a fellow who could sing a song once and make it an overnight hit. Today he could be getting fifty thousand dollars—maybe a hundred thousand a year—and he turned his back on all that for the bottle."

Whenever Lawrence encounters excessive drinking among his boys he is upset. As one of them says: "We're in for a lecture."

How or why certain people become virtual slaves of John Barleycorn makes Lawrence shake his head in bafflement. "And it seems to me," he says, "that they always choose the very worst time for their bouts—maybe just before an important audition, or special broadcast. They go right ahead even though they know it means losing a job, or even losing their union card."

But Lawrence does speak with a certain sympathy of a friend of his who found alcohol his bête noir.

For several years in a row Lawrence traveled with this man in the close association of the business, and, says the maestro earnestly: "He was a talented musician and a fine man. I looked up to him a lot, and thought of him as a good friend."

Lawrence remembers now that they never had a drink together until one fatal day. Then it was the bandleader himself who suggested that they step out for "a few beers." His friend demurred, but Lawrence urged: "Oh, come on. Let's celebrate. It's my birthday. That's only once a year."

They had those few drinks together, and afterward Lawrence returned to his lodgings and went to bed for the night. Not so the other man. He lingered in the tavern and helped close it up at 2 A.M. Moreover, he brought back a bottle to drink in his room. What happened subsequently was devastating.

Lawrence's friend, whom he "looked up to," zoomed off on a wild alcoholic spree.

"That finished him with the band," Lawrence says. "I felt awful about it."

The incident had a sequel.

Some years later, while on a tour, quite by accident Lawrence bumped into his old friend, now obviously sober.

"What in the world happened to you that time?" Lawrence asked.

The man had this to say: "I shouldn't have taken that first drink. I had to find out the hard way that I'm one of those fellows who just can't touch the stuff. You won't know what I'm talking about, but I tell you if I take so much as a sip I'm off. Just one drink sets up a nervous craving that drives me literally nuts."

They were walking down the main street of the town as the man spoke, and he pointed to the window of a liquor store they were passing: "See that plate glass," he said. "Well, if I took a drink right now and then couldn't get another, I wouldn't guarantee what I'd do. I might behave OK, but then again I might break through that window to steal a bottle. See what I mean when I say I gotta steer clear of the stuff."

Of late years Lawrence says, "I've found out about Alcoholics Anonymous. That's the best thing I know of to show fellows like that they can stop and how to do it, if they want to."

Lawrence himself very rarely takes a drink. "I don't like the taste of the stuff," he declares.

Apparently he never did like it, for one of his old associates remembers today: "During the Prohibition era when I was with Lawrence, it was quite the thing for some guy in the audience who liked our orchestra to come backstage and pass a flask around. Just so he wouldn't hurt anybody's feelings, Lawrence would take it and put it to his lips but he didn't fool me. He didn't take a sip."

Of late years Lawrence has had a medical excuse for not drinking, namely the gall-bladder condition which necessitated his 1952 operation.

Since many people don't know this, Lawrence constantly receives gifts of fancy firewater, especially champagne. The cabinet in the Welks' recreation room is crammed with everything from absinthe to crème de menthe, from Napoleon brandy to cognac.

After Shirley and Dr. Robert Fredericks were married (in 1954), Fern found that her new son liked an occasional drink, so she told him to help himself, and she ended with the remark that hit Bob's funny bone. She complained wearily: "Oh, that stuff just keeps piling up down there!" As he was about to offer her his condolences, she topped her first remark with: "Go on down now and help yourself. Take a little of everything."

Bob could only exclaim: "That would be the day! 'A little of everything' and I can just see Dad Welk shipping me—and a king-size hangover—to Siberia, on a one-way ticket."

Ah, wine, women, and song!—which brings up another headache that Lawrence has had to contend with at times, "women trouble."

"If a man's home life isn't as it should be, he won't be any good for the band," the leader says. "And bad love affairs, especially, spoil a man's playing by making him jumpy and nervous."

Why? Well, illicit love affairs in real life aren't like romantic movie dramas. They are often carried on in cheap hotels, hidden on some back street, and under a pall of shame and fear of discovery—enough reason for jumpiness. But the Music Maker adds quickly: "Fortunately, we don't have that kind of man in the band."

"That the maestro gets and keeps upright people shows that he knows how to select and handle men," says one of the Welkmen.

Another clue? Could be.

But how does he "handle," and get along with, his boys on a day-to-day basis?

♫

Chapter 18

"Hail, Hail, the Gang's All Here"

"It's a surprising trait that crops out after you get to know the man, but Lawrence has a streak of waggery in his make-up. He's like the kid who brought the toy mouse home to scare the wits out of old Aunt Lizzie, or put the dead frog in Sis's bed. He enjoys pulling innocent jokes." So says one of the boys.

Shortly after Maurice Pearson joined the band, the lad bought a used car. It was neither a Dodge nor Plymouth. "Don't tell the boss," he pleaded with several Welkmen. "He might give me a hard time, especially since I got stuck with a piece of junk."

But somehow news gets around and one afternoon a few days later, when the boy was in the Santa Monica office, Lawrence announced to the assembled personnel: "Jack Minor of Dodge Company phoned me today. He says they have a new car that they'll sell at less than cost—around twelve hundred dollars. Somebody ordered a four-door, and this two-door was sent by mistake, so it's on their hands."

He paused and glanced at Maurice. The boy was a sickly green. He had paid eight hundred for his six-year-old junk pile.

"How much down?" a stenographer asked.

"A hundred dollars," Lawrence replied.

Maurice gulped audibly. He had put three hundred dollars down.

"How much per week?" another person inquired.

"Oh, not much, just . . ." Lawrence began.

At this point Maurice couldn't stand it a second longer. He got up and left the room. It was some time later when he found out that Lawrence had been "pulling at his leg," and no such fabulous bargain existed.

But the trait most often remarked in regard to Lawrence's attitude with the boys is an almost paternal solicitude.

"Lawrence is a sort of father-confessor," one of them puts it. "Although he's been on the job all day, and although he's to play again at night at the Aragon, he's never too tired to listen to you, or too busy to help you. You can go to him with all your headaches from your mother-in-law to your mortgage payments."

If a few of the boys dub this "excessive interest" or "interference" in their private lives, and complain about Lawrence's repetitiousness, his smugness, his Puritanism, and his triteness, the great majority take a different tack. They say: "There's only one Lawrence Welk. Never saw a guy like him. All in all, he's the best boss in the world."

Then a few of the boys will go on to recount little case histories to prove their point.

There's the Case of the Musician and the Operation. It happened in the days when the band was smaller and each member indispensable to its proper functioning. A certain musician badly needed an operation, but he felt that he simply must postpone it. Another man in the band was al-

ready out ill, and two coincidental replacements seemed
unthinkable. How would Lawrence ever manage? The
man reckoned without his boss. Apprised of the situation,
the bandleader decreed: "Your health comes first. Go
ahead with the operation."

And when the man protested: "Oh, I wouldn't do that
to you, Lawrence," his boss shot back: "Get that operation
now, or you're fired."

Then, to cap the climax, Lawrence, who was not a man
of fabulous wealth in those days, insisted upon taking care
of the man's hospital and doctor bills.

George Cates, Lawrence's musical supervisor, tells a tale
to match. Call it Case History No. 2. After he had been
with the band about a year, he suffered a heart attack
and was laid up for three months. Lawrence mailed him
weekly pay checks just as though he were on the job, and
furthermore billed him on the show as though credit for it
were due him.

"You don't forget that kind of thing," asserts Mr. Cates.
"The loyalty that Lawrence inspires is half his secret."

Another of Lawrence's boys expresses a similar idea:
"You want to work for a boss who gives you your share,
and more, of the spotlight. You want to give him all you've
got."

Still another associate puts it: "Lawrence is never a big
shot with anybody. He never pulls rank."

Perhaps it is when Lawrence's interest in the boys
touches the romantic, or moral, aspect of man's life that an
occasional discordant note may be struck.

Case histories? Nobody in the band supplies them, but
Lawrence himself tells of good-intentioned maneuvers

which conceivably, though not certainly, might have rubbed some fellow the wrong way.

Years ago he had a homely Harry in the band, whom the girls always seemed to pass by. When Lawrence called "Ladies Choice" and invited women on the dance floor to pick their partners from the band members, this masculine wallflower was invariably left unplucked. One night the band was playing in a South Dakota town where a beauty-contest winner, Miss South Dakota, lived. She showed up at the ballroom, and our homely friend kept eying her wistfully from afar.

Hoping to boost the morale of his musician, Lawrence phoned the girl the next day, and asked: "How about doing me a favor? How about phoning our sax player? It would make him feel mighty good. Just ask him to stop by to see you and say good-by before the band leaves town."

There's a bit of characteristic Welkese.

On second thought, though, the actions which contain moral meat are perhaps more characteristic, like the story of . . . well, let X be his name.

X, a married man (no longer with the band), had a girl friend of the more intimate variety. Lawrence talked to the fellow, but he wasn't sure how potent his warnings were. At any rate, because a new engagement took the band to another city, the affair broke off. It was then that the maestro learned through the grapevine that the girl was to have a baby. He decided to teach X a lesson and thus discourage future transgressions. Lawrence arranged with an amiable policeman to apprehend the boy and tell him peremptorily that he was wanted in the town he had just left, on the charge of evading paternity of Miss Y's child.

X blanched and began to stammer protests: "There were other men. She was running around with lots of fellows. Why pick on me?" etc., etc.

"Tell it to the judge," cut in the officer. "My orders are to arrest you."

"Can't I talk to my boss before you cart me off?" the fellow asked between tremors.

Consent was grudgingly given, and X rushed over to Lawrence, begging: "Don't let this get to my wife. Tell her anything, but don't tell her why I'm in jail."

Lawrence was very grave. He listened without comment at first, but in the end he said: "I'll do more than that. I'll speak to that policeman and see if there's a way I can get you released, provided you promise to lead a good life from now on."

The boy promised. Whether or not he kept the promise nobody knows. Lawrence naïvely assumes that most surely he did.

The fact that nearly all of his boys enjoy the blessing of a happy home is a source of deep satisfaction to Lawrence. "And it shows in their faces," he declares. "When we go on tour, I have people all over the country tell me: 'Your group looks so happy.' That's just because they're doing right."

Lawrence knows the wives and children of his boys and, despite his busy schedule, manages to have occasional get-togethers with them.

Since the relationship of Lawrence and the boys is personal and intimate, it is not surprising that he takes a great deal of care in selecting his crew. Then if he finds a musician he wants, it is doubtful that he would let the man get away from him. Take the story of Buddy Merrill's hiring . . .

After Buddy was the winner of a special contest, The Lawrence Welk All-American Competition (held in 1955), Lawrence decided that the boy might be a good addition to the band. When the winds wafted the hint of Lawrence's genuine interest to Buddy, the boy was a mighty thrilled, but at the same time a mighty upset, kid. It was a fantastically fortunate opportunity, but . . . he had not finished high school. He certainly didn't want to turn down the chance of a lifetime, but he did long for that diploma that he'd worked for throughout almost twelve years of schooling. Buddy bounced around on the uncomfortable horns of this dilemma for a while because he did not know Lawrence Welk. When Lawrence realized Buddy's predicament, he made the decision for the boy. He said: "Go ahead, finish school. I'll keep the job open for you."

Lawrence doesn't seem to go about hiring men in an orthodox manner. For instance, he doesn't emphasize experience. When he was about to take on one of his younger boys, somebody in his organization protested: "Why pick an unknown kid? You're paying him big money. For that kind of dough, you could get the best pro in the business."

"But good pros can always get a top-notch job," Lawrence retorted. "This kid, because he's green, may not land much right off. He's real good. I like him and I want to give him a chance."

On the other hand, Lawrence will not readily give a chance to a man who asks for it on the plea: "I belong to the same church you do, Mr. Welk."

Says Lawrence: "That's wrong. We shouldn't use our

religion to trade with. Lots of my boys don't go to my church, and I wouldn't want them to, if they went just to butter me up."

Character and decency are Lawrence's first requirements—then talent. Therefore, he looks at each musician as a man, never as a part of a mass, or as a unit in a category of violinists, or pianists, fellow churchmen, or what have you.

One of the boys expresses it this way: "I'm not just a trombone player to Lawrence. I'm Pete Lofthouse, who happens to play the trombone."

Such an approach inspires more of that loyalty which George Cates spoke of.

Lawrence will advise his boys with all their problems; he will hospitalize them if they need it; he will aid and abet their romances, he will take them to a priest, minister, or rabbi if a marriage needs straightening out, but—come to think of it—there is one thing he won't do. He will never lend them money—or hardly ever.

"You make enemies lending money, and you don't do the people any good, either," he declares. "Often a person can't pay the money back and then instead of blaming himself, he gets mad at you, and at the whole world. Or if he can pay back, he'll probably ask you for more money the next year, and he'll be sore if you refuse the second loan. If you keep lending money to people, you have a bad condition: after a while, they think you owe it to them. So you've hurt their character, and independence."

Nor is Lawrence particularly prone to give his boys money—in cash. Even the very handsome bonuses he presents at Christmas are usually in the form of insurance policies or securities, which Lawrence feels will not be spent so quickly as cash.

"People spend too fast today," Lawrence declares. "You can't build up big and substantial that way."

With regard to bonuses he confesses: "Sometimes I like to give a little extra to a real deserving fellow, but if I do, I can't let on to the other boys. They might be envious. Some of my advisers tell me I shouldn't give extras. I don't see that. We shouldn't let envy stop our generosity. It's right to be real generous for some reason not every outsider sees, as long as we give everybody his due."

The securities Lawrence does give his boys he hopes will be held, or be reinvested and made to increase. "Everybody who works should try to put up a little for a rainy day," he opines. "We never know when that day will come, and we shouldn't expect Uncle Sam, who only has to take the money from the pockets of our friends and neighbors, to look after us."

Lawrence carries his idea of investment and saving so far that he has encouraged an investment club, started and managed by accordionist Myron Floren. The plan is that every member invest a set sum each week, the total to be used for the purchase of securities listed on the New York Stock Exchange.

The club has grown very rapidly. In 1956, the year it began, there were seventeen members owning $12,000 worth of stock. Then a second club was formed for newer members who preferred to invest smaller sums. By January 1957, B Club had a total of twenty-one members, since some of the boys were members of both clubs. Anyone can sell out as he desires, but so far that has happened only once or twice.

Lawrence Welk's boys like being capitalists.

But none of them was a capitalist in 1934. Wasn't that where the story left off?

♫

Chapter 19

"I Get Ideas"

When the Texas interlude had ended, a few zigzag jaunts led eventually to Yankton and familiar station WNAX for the second engagement there. The band this time was billed as The Hotsy Totsy Boys.

"Isn't that an awful name?" Lawrence practically blushes about it now.

It was during this Yankton engagement that the band-leader bought his electrical appliance store, and doubled as shopkeeper for a few hours following the morning broadcasts, some mornings when he could spare the time from the band.

Says a Welk enthusiast: "Lawrence never lets anything come before the band. If I had to name the one major quality which accounts for his success, it would be that business of keeping his eye on the ball, and on his long-range plans. Regardless of every other demand on his time and attention, he never allows his mind to stray far from music."

Ever on the lookout then for anything or anybody that might improve the band, he was pleased as punch when organist Jerry Burke crossed his path. "I knew who he was," Lawrence says, "because his older brother played banjo and guitar with me while Jerry was still in high school. Now I found out that he was real good, and I had an idea that he would help the band. I decided to hire him."

Although Lawrence is a hard person to turn down, once he asks a person to do something, the fact that Jerry accepted the bandleader's offer can best be explained by the esteem in which the organist held his prospective boss. He says: "I was making seventy-five dollars a week with a co-op band—pretty good wages for the Depression. The prevailing scale of forty a week less was the salary that Lawrence could pay me."

Evidently Jerry knew what he was doing when he agreed to go along with Mr. Music Maker. Today he claims: "That was the smartest decision I ever made."

He holds a record with the Lawrence Welk band: he has worked with it longer than any other member—twenty-four years. Also that must be some sort of record in the business, for most musicians change jobs almost as often as they buy a new suit of clothes.

As Lawrence added to his band, and made improvements generally, his reputation grew, his plans expanded, and new ideas came to him.

The band traveled a great deal, and a group of eight men crowded into a seven-passenger car (with their instruments strapped to the top), besides not making for comfort, posed another problem. The very weight caused the tires to blow out. Lawrence tried to solve the latter problem by having the car lengthened, but the crowding, the discomfort, and the lack of rest, remained. What could he do about them?

One bleak, raw morning, traveling along the highway,

Lawrence looked around at his little group of sleepy musicians, drooping in their seats, and asked unnecessarily: "Are you fellows tired?"

A weak voice from the back seat piped up: "I wouldn't exactly say tired, but two vultures have been following us for the last hundred miles."

The other men should have presented that fellow with a medal if it was his remark that inspired Lawrence's next idea. He decided to build a trailer bus of his own, have it fitted up as a sleeper with folding bunks installed along the sides, so that the boys could rest during their nocturnal journeyings. He even hired a man to do the driving. While the man drove the boys slept; while they played he slept.

"I'm not sure," says Lawrence, "but I think maybe we invented the sleeper bus. It is used quite a lot now by traveling orchestras."

His next idea was certainly a novel one too, though it concerned a far different kind of thing than bus travel. Lawrence noticed that the highest-paid bands were usually the sponsored ones, so he declares: "That was what I wanted next—a sponsor."

The question was how to get one. That he could not find a firm willing to consider the band was no reason to forget the idea, not according to Lawrence. "Never say die," might well be his motto, and a recurring clue.

Anyway he says: "When I couldn't talk anybody into sponsoring us, I decided to become my own sponsor."

Now that may sound like something *Alice in Wonderland's* duchess might have dreamed up, yet Lawrence managed it. He ordered huge quantities of chewing gum, wrapped in paper labeled "Honolulu Fruit Gum." Then he had painted upon his bus in giant red and green letters:

"LAWRENCE WELK AND HIS HONOLULU FRUIT GUM BAND," and wherever the band played, there was an announcement from the bandstand: "Lawrence Welk and his orchestra, sponsored by Honolulu Fruit Gum."

But that was only the beginning. As one of Lawrence's Hollywood cronies says: "The man is instinctively a showman. He has a flare for putting things across."

At his nightly dances Mr. Music Maker gave out free gum and held popularity contests of all sorts. Patrons could vote in the contests by writing on the gum wrapper. There was no limit to the number of votes a person might cast, provided each vote was written on a separate gum wrapper.

Some of the contests were for a Miss South Dakota, a Miss Nebraska, etc. And were some of the contests for favorite bands and musicians? And did some people vote for the Lawrence Welk band? At any rate, as though a sorcerer's wand had been waved over the Midwest, making the inhabitants suddenly Welk-conscious, so the notion of contests seemed to work. Evidently, too, the public reasoned that, if the band were good enough for a sponsor, it must be really good, and they wanted it to play for them.

"On account of the demand, we could get higher pay," the leader points out.

All very neat! Ingenious—and at the same time ingenuous. Lawrence Welk is one person who proves that the two qualities are not always mutually exclusive.

But ideas continued to come. Why not make money directly from the gum? As a preliminary, he began to put out gum of varying flavors, so that soon the wrappers bore the words: "Lawrence Welk's Spearmint," or "Lawrence Welk's Peppermint," or "Lawrence Welk's Cinnamon

Gum," etc.; then he hired several men (one of them being old George T. Kelly, of Peerless Entertainers days) as traveling salesmen to distribute his product.

Eventually, however, as might have been expected, some snags appeared. First, a national chewing-gum manufacturer claimed that Lawrence's wrapper infringed on his, and threatened to file suit. Second, ballroom operators began to wail loudly: after every Welk dance, they had to scrape their floors, and then call in the refinishers.

Lawrence decided that his chewing-gum venture must inevitably die the death. *"Requiescat in pace!"*

"I didn't feel too bad," he states. "It had lasted long enough to help a lot. The band was better known and better paid."

Engagements were plentiful. Constant one-night stands throughout the north Midwest kept the band on the go. Popularity seemed to snowball.

Also (since more musicians were employed) the band grew bigger, and Lawrence began to feel that it was ready to go on to a bigger city and do bigger things.

Chapter 20

♫

"What'll I Do?"

In the fall of 1936 Lawrence and the band went to Omaha.

Today that city reminds him of three things: another business venture, a new baby, and his bus carrying him into a period of uncertainty.

But first why did he go to Omaha?

"I guess it was one of those impetuous moves that Fern says I used to make," Lawrence admits, "but I got real excited when some friend kept talking to me about a great opportunity for the band there. Omaha is a lot bigger than Yankton, so I figured that we were on our way to bigger things. Right away I sold the store and our Yankton house, and bought a home near Omaha. It was on the highway out from town and it had a nice little piece of ground around it, too—about three acres, where I planned to raise chickens as a side-line business."

This particular commercial venture might have boosted the family exchequer. Lawrence went about it very scientifically with all the latest methods and equipment, and he hired a man to look after details. However, a certain habit of his drained off profits. He would say to his boys, and to everybody else he met: "We're raising chickens.

Stop by the place some afternoon, and we'll give you a couple."

They stopped by in droves.

Meanwhile the music business also suffered a setback, and that's why his bus continued to be so important. Lawrence encountered union red tape. It seems that the union there had a rule that a man, though belonging to a national union, must also join the local union, and there is a certain "sweating out" period while the man must wait for his local card before he can work in that jurisdiction.

"I couldn't just sit around in Omaha and wait," Lawrence explains. "According to the rules, I could accept jobs in the outlying districts, so that's what I did."

It meant constant one-night stands, and riding the sleeper bus again. Only the expected baby could break the monotonous pattern.

Returning home on a certain night, after one of his expeditions, Lawrence was met at the door by a woman the Welks had planned to have take care of Shirley during Fern's confinement. The presence of the outsider indicated that Mrs. Welk had already gone to the hospital. Mrs. Schroeder, the wife of Lawrence's agent at the time, had driven her there.

"I rushed over real quick," Lawrence recounts, "but I couldn't see Fern. She was in the delivery room. I just had to wait. While I was waiting, I happened to get talking to this doctor, and right off I let myself in for something, because I was breathing sort of raspy."

The doctor diagnosed pleurisy and prescribed hospitalization for Lawrence too.

Fern was on one floor, Lawrence was on another. He kept asking the nurse every few minutes how things were going on the maternity floor. He says: "It seemed a long time before they told me that it was over. Fern was all right, and it was a girl."

When he did receive this word, it was literally too much for him to "take lying down." He wanted to see his wife and daughter. What matter that he was running a fever? Watching his chance to elude the nurses, he stole from bed and upstairs to Fern's floor. He wasn't sure of her room number, but he easily found the nursery and took a peek through the glass partition. Scrutinizing the occupants of the tiny cribs, he picked out an infant he felt sure was his own, and although he didn't burst into song with "Yes Sir, That's My Baby," he did startle a passer-by with the excited cry: "That's my baby over there! The one with the pretty ears."

As a musician, Lawrence would expect his offspring to have a good ear—or ears. But he had guessed correctly.

For the little girl born that February day of 1937 he wrote his song, "My Donna Lee." But the creative effort did not interfere with his bus-riding existence. That resumed the minute he left the hospital.

It was like Yankton doubled and redoubled. Every night a new place; every dawn the long ride home.

It was during this sleeper-bus era that an accident occurred which in turn led to perplexity and doubt.

Late one afternoon the band was hurrying toward a playing date, at Esterville, Iowa. Despite the lingering daylight some of the boys were resting in their bunks, and Lawrence himself was trying to get a little of the sleep so hard to find time for in his business. Suddenly the thing happened. The spindle broke, the wheels locked, and the clumsy vehicle lurched crazily, then with surprising speed, crashed down an eighteen-foot embankment into a ditch, where it lay like a dead elephant.

Lawrence describes the incident today in some detail: "I was in my bunk at the time, but I was thrown to one end of the bus. Maybe I was knocked out a minute. I don't know for sure. I remember feeling sort of dazed and smelling gasoline real strong. But then it dawned on me that that could mean fire. Scared as a jack rabbit, I jumped up and crawled through the window. Some of the fellows had been thrown clear out of the bus. There, on the highway, were bodies. All I could think of was: Is anybody hurt bad? I ran from one to another. I could see blood on a couple —Leo Fortin, and Terry George. I thought they were dead, and I tried to pray. There were a lot of people around. Where all the people came from, I don't know, but we were on a pretty busy highway. Some cops were there too. I guess they must have been the ones who called the ambulance. We got Leo and Terry on that."

Before these two men were rushed to the hospital, Lawrence learned that they were not dead, as he had feared. In fact, it developed that even their injuries were not very serious.

The policemen on the scene drove the rest of the group into town. They were a bedraggled lot, scarred with a few cuts and bruises of their own. They had been wearing overalls to travel in, and these were saturated with gasoline and in some cases torn and muddy. The rest of their clothes remained behind in suitcases stored in the wrecked bus.

"We had a date that night—the one we were heading for when the accident happened," Lawrence says. "I phoned the ballroom operator when I got in town, but he didn't want to hear about the accident. The only thing that worried him was whether we'd show up for the dance. And he was kind of sore about us being two men short."

None of the boys felt like playing, but they did play—and in their torn, muddy overalls. They had nothing to change into.

"We must have looked funny," Lawrence admits. "And there were Band-Aids—and even big bandages on some of the fellows."

Moreover, Lawrence remembers: "The band didn't sound so good. I was awful glad when we finished up—2 A.M. never seemed so long in coming before, because all the boys were exhausted. I was myself, but I was so upset that I couldn't sleep."

For some time Lawrence remained upset. The accident lived in his mind as a vivid horror. He would frequently wake in the night and the whole scene, accompanied by the sound effects of the screeching ambulance sirens, would re-enact itself.

Although nobody was hurt very seriously, he felt guilty that anybody in his employ should have been hurt at all. For the first time since the opening year of his career when the trumpeter had lampooned his playing, Lawrence considered giving up the music business. Since Shirley's birth he had tried to keep a foot in both camps—music and a commercial enterprise, but what he thought of doing now was different. He really faced up to the idea of abandoning music completely.

To do it would mean a fearful wrench, so there followed the time of crisis, the time during which Lawrence had to answer the perplexing and painful question: What'll I do?

Maybe the period was short-lived, but it was long enough.

"I really prayed hard to know what to do," Lawrence avows, "but I stayed in the dark. Well, I had been taught that God doesn't usually reach out of heaven to whisper things right in our ears. He oftener works through humans like ourselves, so I decided to talk my problem over with our parish priest."

To Lawrence's surprise he was told: "You have no moral obligation to give up music. Sure, you had an accident, but there are hazards inherent in the process of living. Since there was no palpable negligence, don't blame yourself."

Lawrence walked out of the rectory with a lighter step than he had managed in weeks. Then he went home that evening to hear five-year-old Shirley adding to her night prayers: "Please, dear God, don't let the bus go over in a ditch any more."

The priest's opinion and Shirley's prayer would probably have been enough, but on top of them came the offer of a booking in Denver's Rainbow Ballroom. These three, converging in point of time, effectively laid Lawrence's scruples to rest.

Today he will set forth as an important rule of success: "Find something you love, and then stick to it. Everybody can do one thing real well, but nobody can do a lot of things just right."

But did Lawrence disregard his own advice? When so challenged, he reacted with shocked surprise: "Oh, I thought about giving up music, and at times I had other businesses, but in the meantime I always stuck to music. And when in the very beginning, I picked music, I picked it only because I loved it. I often work sixteen or eighteen hours a day. People ask me how I do it. I can do it because, like Fern says, my work is my recreation too."

Indeed she goes further, declaring: "If Lawrence didn't love his work, it would kill him."

That is not hard to believe, after a few spot checks of his grueling schedule. Take the trip to Washington for the presidential inauguration. He left California on the night of January 20, after performing at the Aragon Ballroom at Ocean Park. His plane landed in Washington the next morning. That means he had to sit up all night, dozing as best he could.

The arrival time was 11:05 A.M., and from 11:10 on, when he had an appointment to pose for photos, it was one appointment after another all day long, ending in the late afternoon (4:30), when he saw Drs. White and Walsh about his nomination as commander in chief of the Heart Fund's March of a Million scheduled for February 24.

At a few minutes before 5 P.M. he went to his hotel room for an interval of about an hour, supposedly reserved to check factual data for this book with Mary Lewis Coakley. During that work, Les Kauffman, one of his staff, ordered a light dinner sent up for Lawrence. It consisted of bouillon, sandwich, and custard; it was the only meal the bandleader had a chance to eat between then and breakfast the next morning.

As he ate, also answering questions for his biographer, the phone kept ringing. Though Les answered it, it was always for Lawrence, and Lawrence always took the call.

Les cut up the sandwich, and handed it to Lawrence in bits, as the latter held the phone and listened. One woman called up to say: "I got you the bid to play for the Inaugural Balls. I wrote a letter to Congress suggesting you. I want you to get me a bid to one of the balls."

Another phoned to tell him: "I knew you when you played in St. Paul. I wasn't married then, and now would you believe it, I have five children! I thought you'd like to hear from an old fan."

To all Lawrence was unfailingly polite, and he ended each conversation with: "Thank you for calling. It was nice to talk to you."

(Who spoke of Lawrence's never-tiring courtesy as a clue?)

When Lawrence finished those phone calls and his dinner, he had to hurry to a cocktail party at the Sheraton Park Hotel (for ABC personnel, disc jockeys, and the press); he had to meet the governor of North Dakota; and he had to find time to dress in tails before the eight-o'clock rehearsal, preceding his nine-thirty performance at the first inaugural ball, also at the Sheraton Park.

Parenthetically, the full-dress suit Lawrence wore that night was rented at the last minute before he left California. He didn't have time to buy one, and he explains: "A couple of months before—along with most of my suits— I gave away my tails to the Hungarian Clothing Drive. I figured they would keep some poor fellow warm anyhow."

That night he played at three of the four inaugural balls, that is he played at the Sheraton Park, at the Mayflower, and at the Armory. He was scheduled to go on to the Statler, for the remaining inaugural ball. However, because his replacement orchestra was late in arriving at the Mayflower, the latter part of the schedule was thrown off, and through no fault of his own Lawrence never did make the last destination.

He finished up at the Armory between 2:30 and 3 A.M., returned to his room at the Mayflower, changed into a business suit, and left for the National Airport. A special plane landed him in New York between 5 and 6 A.M., where he checked into the Warwick Hotel. (N.B.: Only a short morning nap, but no sleep that night.)

During the day he had to make six New York interviews, set up for him with ABC personnel, script writers, publicity men, etc. At 12:40 the next morning, he left New York for Wichita, Kansas, and thence on to Los Angeles. He arrived in time to take over the rehearsal for his forthcoming Saturday-night show, thus relieving Myron Floren, who is an occasional substitute leader.

Since its beginning Lawrence never missed a single network show, until he took his first vacation from it, in the midsummer of 1957. "To tell the truth," Lawrence admits, "that was not only my first vacation from ABC, it was the first vacation I ever took since I had a band of my own."

It lasted a meager two weeks. In that time limit he and Fern flew cross-country to New York, and thence to Europe and back again. How much could he really have seen of London, Paris, Rome? And he never glimpsed the German/French town of Strasbourg, whose progeny was responsible for little Strasburg, North Dakota.

Then, before he could leave on the trip, he worked literally around the clock, to set up programs to be shown on kinescope in his absence. (Incidentally, that is the one instance of Lawrence using kinescope. At all other times his show comes "live" from Hollywood.)

But he loves the life, every minute of it!

He loved it back in 1937, when, shortly after Donna was born, he set out for Denver. The Rainbow Ballroom, where he was to play, was owned by O. K. Farr. He and his wife, now living in California, have maintained a friendship with Lawrence and Fern from that date to this.

Of their first meeting Lawrence says: "I was glad to play for Mr. Farr, a real nice fellow," and he adds: "I figured that the Rainbow would be a good steppingstone to the big things I always dreamed about."

But before he actually saw his dream take on any semblance of reality, he had to experience a few more struggles —or even, it might be said, a long crisis, in which his career seemed to hang in the balance, swinging first this way and then that.

Chapter 21

♫

"See-Saw"

Like a seesaw came success, failure; and success, failure again.

St. Paul, Minnesota, which (after the interposition of a few one-nighters) followed Denver, was a success, and even today Lawrence tells about it in an exultant tone.

He was playing for a few nights' run at a town about thirty-five miles from St. Paul. During his free daytime hours, on one particular day, he brought the band into the city for lunch at the Lowery Hotel. Enjoying the quiet, dignified atmosphere of the place, which contrasted favorably with the hurly-burly of some of the ballrooms on their recent route, Lawrence remarked, strictly as a joke: "I'm going to book you fellows in a hotel like this."

Everybody laughed and, being in a relaxed mood, continued the banter. As they left the Lowery, and were walking down the street, they saw a block or so away the St. Paul Hotel. "Might as well begin now," Lawrence said. "I'll go in here, and come out with a booking."

Actually, because he knew the manager of the hotel, a Mr. Calhoun, he did decide to stop by and say hello. But did he also figure "Nothing ventured, nothing gained," when in the course of the conversation with his friend he asked (still in the joking manner, to be sure): "When are you going to book us here?"

Mr. Calhoun replied: "When can you start to work?"

To Mr. Music Maker's ears the tone sounded serious. He shot back: "You mean that?"

"Sure I do," came the response.

"Oh-h," gasped Lawrence, and then, quickly recovering his poise, he added: "I'll let you know what I can arrange."

As usual he was booked up with scattered engagements through many weeks ahead. But this opportunity was too good to turn down, if there were any possible way of seizing it. Leaving Mr. Calhoun staring after him, he rushed to the nearest phone. Quickly he called ballroom operators who had engaged the band, and asked them if they would release him temporarily on his promise to give them a future booking. At last he fixed it so that he could begin work at the St. Paul in about four weeks.

That booking was important. It was the first hotel ballroom the band had ever played. "It gave us class, and helped us reach real good spots later," Lawrence explains.

As it happened, the manager of the St. Paul knew the manager of the William Penn* in Pittsburgh, and he recommended the Welk orchestra so highly that Lawrence soon found himself on the way to the steel city.

In the seesaw pattern this engagement was a failure. The least said about it the better.

But with a Boston engagement that followed Lawrence soared upward again to success. A booking there in Roy Gill's ballroom meant that the erstwhile Midwestern farm boy had at least cracked the hard East and made a few

* Now the Penn Sheraton.

gentry of a staid metropolis sit up, take notice, and enjoy his gay tunes.

While he was still on that job, his booker, Bill Fredericks (of Fredericks Brothers Music Corporation), came to him one day to announce that the manager of the William Penn in Pittsburgh wanted the band for a second engagement.

Lawrence's answer was: "Now, Bill, please don't kid me. This isn't funny to me. I know we flopped there last time."

"I'm on the level," Bill Fredericks replied. "The manager decided that he'd made a mistake the first time. He put your band in that ornate, formal Italian Room.° It didn't suit your style. This time he's going to put you in the rathskeller. It's a homey, casual setting that he thinks will give you the proper background."

Red-faced and embarrassed at the very remembrance of his other performance in the hotel, Lawrence declared: "I don't want to go."

Bill didn't argue the merits of the place further; instead he changed his tactics: "Lawrence, I didn't know you felt that way, and now I'm on the spot. I already signed a contract for you. Won't you help a guy out and go through with it?"

It was the kind of plea that Lawrence Welk wouldn't refuse.

To this day Lawrence is happy that he did return to Pittsburgh, and he declares: "That engagement was the first real success for our band. Even on Monday, the dullest night of the week, we had the place bursting with peo-

° Now the Terrace Room.

ple. And of course Pittsburgh is a milestone because of something more important."

He is referring to the fact that it was in Pittsburgh during that second engagement that Phil Davis, of radio station WCAE, heard the Welk music and remarked: "It has the sparkle and effervescence of champagne."

"So-o," says Lawrence, "after fifteen years of playing in public, we had a name for our music. It clicked right off."

There, in two words, the fans found a veritable definition of the elusive quality of Welkese melody.

It followed naturally that Lawrence began calling his male trio the Sparklers, and his girl singer the Champagne Lady, and for a signature piece he took a song written years before, made it lighter and bouncier, and called it "Bubbles in the Wine." (It is still the signature piece on the Lawrence Welk show. Now, can't every fan from Maine to California hear its familiar strains on his inner ear?)

Incidentally that song was none other than the tender ballad, originally called "You're My Home Sweet Home," which he had written (and lost money publishing at his own expense) when Shirley was born. In Lawrence's heart, then, Shirley will always be his first Champagne Lady.

On the band the first Champagne Lady was Lois Best, "a real wonderful little girl." She gave up her job when she married Lawrence's trumpet player, Jules Herman. Recently, when the maestro was in Minneapolis, he invited the Hermans (Jules now has his own orchestra, and Lois sings for him) to the stage to perform with the present Champagne Music Makers.

But meantime, back in 1938–39, the term Champagne Music spread rapidly as Lawrence kept touring. To list the places he went to in the next months would be to sound like a train dispatcher, spieling off his litany. En route to any new booking Lawrence always ran in a few one-nighters. This earned extra money and it broke the trip.

As for notable bookings, the next after Pittsburgh was Milwaukee, a reasonable success, and then more notable still the "sad flop" of Chicago's Edgewater Beach Hotel. Unfortunately the latter place cannot be dismissed with just a phrase. It had always been one of the most important spots in Lawrence's private dreamland.

"As a kid back on the farm, I used to listen over our first crystal radio set to Danny Russo's band there," Lawrence recalls. "To go there with a band of my own was a real big ambition for me. When the bid came through, I could hardly believe it. My friend Joe Kayser, of Fredericks Brothers, told me that the band had been booked for a whole summer season."

However, from the very beginning of the engagement, things did not go well. When Lawrence and the band arrived, the manager of the hotel, William Dewey, suggested to the leader: "How about making a little opening talk at the orchestra's debut here?"

To Lawrence that sounded like: "How about cutting your throat?" Throughout the long years up to his day in Chicago, Lawrence Welk of the German accent had never made any kind of speech before an audience. He didn't even announce the numbers the band played. "One of the boys could do that at a dance," he explains, "and when we played a theater, I used to hire a master of ceremonies."

At the very mention of the plan Lawrence could feel the cold perspiration prickling his skin, and when he tried to open his mouth to express misgivings to Mr. Dewey, he found his mouth was painfully dry. "In the end," he says, "I just nodded OK."

With a little help from his henchmen he laboriously wrote out a few hundred words, enough to account for about two minutes' speaking time, and then, like a school-boy, he set himself to the task of memorizing them word for word.

Opening day came as quickly as a movie film sequence, and about as automatically Lawrence found himself before a crowd gathered on the hotel terrace outdoors. Mr. Dewey made a very brief introduction and then stepped back.

Lawrence stood alone. Before him was the crowd, blurred, but fantastic, like a many-headed dragon, whose thousands of eyes were all focused on him. Above was the sky, gray, gloomy, and heavy like a giant's clammy hand, seemingly poised to close in upon the victim himself. Summoning what courage he could, he cleared his throat, and made the desperate plunge with his inimitable: "Ladies and gemamin."

At that instant, with perfect timing, there was a clap of thunder, the clouds above literally burst, and rain in great pelting drops hit him in the face, on the shoulders—all over. As fast as its collective legs would carry it, the audience before him scattered in a disorderly scramble for the doorways.

Lawrence remained just where he was.

Doggedly, as though he didn't know what was going on, he began his speech, and as doggedly continued with it to the very end. By the time he had finished, not a person, not even one of his musicians or a stray waiter, remained in sight.

Lawrence, looking like a plucked chicken with his drenched white summer suit clinging to him, admitted: "That beginning wasn't so good."

In the weeks that followed he had to admit that the rest of the engagement "wasn't so good" either. The failure was largely due to his inexperience. Before he had ever played the place, he had gone to the hotel several times, to see how other bands performed there, and he remembered that the leader, between numbers, had approached certain tables and chatted with the more important and distinguished-looking guests. When he came to the Edgewater himself, he was told by the management to play up to a few regular guests of the hotel, for their approval of the band was highly desirable.

Says Lawrence: "Even though I saw what the other leader had done, and even though I heard what the manager said, nothing sank down in my mind. I don't know what was the matter."

Anyway, Lawrence made no special moves toward special people and after he had been at the hotel only a very short time, one of the couples who were permanent guests of the hotel, and whose favor the management wanted particularly to court, remarked to Mr. Dewey that they were disappointed in the Welk orchestra.

Word was passed on to Lawrence through his agent, and he was given to understand that it was more important from the hotel's viewpoint that he please three designated couples instead of a large crowd. Indeed, if he failed to do it, he could expect to receive his notice, and out he would go.

"I was on the spot," Lawrence recalls. "I figured I'd have to move fast. On the night after my agent told me the bad news, I grabbed the bull's horns."

In the intermission between his twenty-minute sets Lawrence went over to the table of the people who had complained about the band, introduced himself, and remarked that he had noticed them there several times. They were gracious and invited him to have a chair and join their party.

He began his conversation with them by saying in all candor: "I started life as a farmer. So to speak, I still have overalls on. This is the first time I ever played a real plush hotel, and I'm a little nervous, because I'm in the darkness about what people like you want me to play. I'd appreciate some suggestions. What tunes would you like to hear?"

They co-operated willingly, and before the evening ended Lawrence had the man up on the bandstand directing the orchestra, while he, Lawrence, danced with the man's wife.

But better still—and without Lawrence's solicitation—that evening the couple left a note under Mr. Dewey's door, reading: "I take back what I said about Lawrence Welk. No doubt he was nervous in the beginning. I would like you to reconsider and keep the orchestra."

However, though he salvaged his job, the engagement did not win him so much as a sprig of fresh laurel for his brow. In fact, as Lawrence says bluntly: "It just about ruined us. We had been getting around five hundred dollars for one-night stands, but when we left the Edgewater Beach, we were lucky if we could get two fifty."

One reason for the debacle was what happened with regard to the "music men" from the song-publishing houses.

Now that Lawrence was in the key spot of the Edgewater and had a network radio show every night, these men came to him and asked him to feature their "plug songs," that is, songs they wanted introduced and pushed for their own commercial interests. Once, while he was at the Edgewater, Lawrence played a fifteen-minute radio program in which he used twelve "plug songs."

Vaguely he realized that he was damaging his reputation by using these new songs, instead of his library of the tested and true numbers, but he did not have the heart to turn down the music men, or the experience to withstand their pressure when they came to him with tears in their eyes and told him that they would lose their jobs if they could not get their songs played on the radio network. "Afterwards I found out," says Lawrence, "that they would get together over a beer, and decide among themselves what sob story to use on me."

When he left the Edgewater Beach, things looked black. There was serious worry that his fiasco at this hotel would mean relegation to the sticks again, and that all his gains of the recent past would be lost.

Here was the very brink of his crisis! He teetered dangerously. His career could go either way.

Chapter 22

♫

"Three Little Words"

Long conferences were held with Lawrence's bookers, L. A. Fredericks and Bill Fredericks. Something had to be done. L.A. knew the manager of the Chicago Theatre. Perhaps there was a way to persuade the fellow to take on the Welk band.

As the talk wove back and forth, Lawrence listened pessimistically. He didn't see how he could climb out of the hole, and even now, on Hollywood's heights, when he recounts that he was indeed booked at the Chicago, a note of wonder creeps into his voice. He says: "How L.A. did it I don't know, because that theater hired only big names. I wasn't one of them. What's more, L.A. arranged so that they would show a top-notch movie during my engagement there."*

Crowds flocked to the Chicago to see the movie, but on the marquee of the theater, beside the title of the picture, appeared a notice of Champagne Music. The Fredericks brothers managed to snap a few photos of the crowds waiting to buy tickets, just as they stood under a sign bearing three words, "Lawrence Welk's Band." These photos

---

* When Lawrence played at a theater in those days, it was customary for him to play on a billing with a movie.

could be used to sell other theater managers on the idea of hiring the orchestra in the future.

"I didn't make such a lot of money on that engagement," Lawrence admits, "but even so, I'll never forget it. It was one of the best."

He has reason to speak so glowingly. The engagement indicated which way this critical passage of his life would eventually be resolved. Meanwhile it also completely counteracted the failure of the Edgewater Beach Hotel and, moreover, it led to an outstanding—in fact a unique —event in the whole Lawrence Welk drama.

Eddie Weisfeldt, manager of the Riverside Theatre in Milwaukee, heard Lawrence and the band at the theater in Chicago. He liked what he heard, but he retained one mental reservation about Lawrence.

After the performance he made his way backstage with a proposition: "Come to Milwaukee," he said, "and I'll put you on at $1750 a week—provided you announce your own numbers."

"But I can't talk," Lawrence protested. "Folks won't understand me."

Mr. Weisfeldt shrugged, picked up his hat, and moved toward the door, then, turning as though to nod good-by, he tossed this small bomb over his shoulder: "Double that —I'll make it $3500 a week."

"What did you say?" stammered Lawrence.

"You heard me," Weisfeldt replied, and closed the door.

In a split second Lawrence had yanked it open again to utter three little words: "I vill talk."

With them he had made the first move to break through his own personal sound barrier!

The follow-up moves were not easy. The speech at the

Edgewater Beach, still fresh in his mind, was a fearful saboteur of morale. He could face a Russian tank just about as easily as he could the microphone.

However, though he began haltingly, his little announcements were well received by his Milwaukee audiences. Accent and all, people rather liked the added touch of his personality to his programs.

He even had women phone him and comment on his "thrilling" speaking voice. He didn't know at the time that, in order to give him a psychological boost, his manager had put them up to that. The scheme boomeranged when one woman told him: "You sound just as good as . . ." and she mentioned the name of another bandleader with a thick accent.

"That really made me feel awful," says Lawrence. "If I was anywhere near as bad as that fellow, I was sure terrible."

To this day Lawrence worries about his mistakes, while at the same time he cherishes a wistful hope of eliminating them.

One afternoon in the summer of 1956 he turned to Lois Lamont, his secretary, and asked: "You've been with us eleven years, Lois, do I talk better now than when you first knew me?"

Lois at first made some evasive reply, but when pressed for an answer she finally spoke up: "Well, if I have to say it—you talk about the same now as the day I met you. You know, you have a mental block. Your very fear that you can't speak English fluently throws up a barrier. But," she added hastily, "don't let it worry you. Your way of speaking is part of your charm."

Maybe she has something there. Most people do seem

to like the individualism of the Welkese language twist. Why even the people whose names Lawrence garbles take it as an amusing and rather endearing quirk, and they will almost boast: "Lawrence calls me such-and-such."

There's the story which has to do with Lois. Her name isn't really Lamont, but a multisyllable moniker, Bielefeldt, which for the life of him Lawrence couldn't remember. Characteristically, he decided that she really should change her name, and he actually had the boys in the band run a contest and vote on the ten best names available. Then the list of these names was handed to Lois for her to make a selection. Before she had a chance to study them, however, Lawrence had occasion to introduce someone to her. He began: "May I present you to my secretary, Miss—er—Miss Lamont."

"Out of the nowhere, into the blue" came Lamont. And apparently it is here to stay.

But then almost anything can happen with Welk and words.

One night he announced his Champagne Music as Shampoo Music. Another night he announced the song "Standing on the Corner" as "Standing around the Corner," and then, realizing that he had made a mistake, hastily corrected it by saying "Standing in the Corner." And he always calls the song entitled "Dry Bones" the "Rib Song," and he has been known to refer to the microphone as microscope.

The speech stories are as thick as Hollywood's bright lights, for Lawrence not only makes occasional speech blunders, he is also at times quite baffled by the correct speech of other people. Jerry Burke tells about the time a newspaper write-up dubbed Lawrence "an infinitesimal nonentity." Jerry, who is very fond of Lawrence, resented it a little, and passed the newspaper to the maestro, pointing out the gibe. Lawrence read it and nodded gravely. A couple of days later he approached Jerry and asked: "What do those words mean—'infinitesimal nonentity'?" Jerry explained, and Lawrence, a trifle miffed, demanded: "Why don't you tell me when they say bad things like that about me?"

Despite all this the Weisfeldt command to talk was equivalent to the order: "Forward march—on the double." Did Lawrence realize that back there in Milwaukee in 1939–40, when he signified that he was falling in step with his three little words: "I vill talk"?

Chapter 23

♫

"Smilin' Through"

Still playing just a little longer the seesaw game, Lawrence had one more serious failure to undergo before he could balance himself on a more or less permanent higher level and feel that the crisis was definitely past. The failure was in the Tower Theatre in Kansas City, Missouri.

There was a reason for it. Champagne Music was not known in Kansas City because Lawrence's broadcasts had never reached the place. Audiences then were pitifully small, and financial rewards worse than nonexistent. Lawrence was engaged on a percentage basis, and there were not sufficient profits to make his share large enough to cover the salaries of his musicians and other expenses. He lost $2200. "That was the biggest amount of money I ever lost in one week," he declares.

However, he could sing "Smilin' Through" because the sad picture was relieved with amusing incidents.

The first day in the city he was walking along the street toward the theater where his band was to play, and at the distance of a block or so away he saw a long line of people apparently waiting to buy tickets.

"It looked like a miracle," he describes it. "I didn't expect that crowd in a town where nobody knew us."

It meant that he could make "lots of money," a welcome prospect at any time. He stood there foolishly grinning as his thought spun on, then he noticed that he had stopped before a haberdasher's shop, flaunting large signs on which was printed the single word "SALE." It occurred to him that he was low on shirts and ties, and on shoes and socks. Why not stock up at bargain prices?

He proceeded to do just that. Then, carrying his bulky package containing his purchases, he went on his way. He hadn't walked more than a few yards when he almost dropped the package in consternation. "Those people—that beautiful, long line of people—were not waiting for tickets to our theater, but to a theater next door to it that I hadn't noticed before. It was playing a real, real popular sea picture."

Later that day the band opened to a very straggly audience. Lawrence didn't need anybody to tell him that there would be no profits from which he might draw a share. In fact, if this went on, he would need every cent of cash he could lay his hands on to pay his expenses.

Why, oh why, did he have to squander that money on clothes?

And about that opening show, it was enough in itself to turn his hair gray. In telling what happened Lawrence explains that, before the band arrived in Kansas City, the manager of the Tower hinted that he would like some acts to enliven the orchestra's part of the program. Driving through Iowa, on the way to the new assignment, the boys heard of a performing dog, and arranged for the animal's trainer to give a show in the hotel where Lawrence was staying. The dog went through his tricks, and Lawrence admits: "That pooch looked great. I hired the act right off and took it to Kansas City with us."

At the opening performance the orchestra played a few introductory chords, the dog was led to the center of the stage by his trainer, and then the spotlight was put on him. Presto—frightened by the glare, the animal turned tail and made a dash for the wings.

Talk about pandemonium! The maddest of mad scrambles ensued, as everybody in the band, plus a few stagehands as well, tried to catch that elusive bit of frisky, frightened fox terrier—without success.

Just as the mounting blood pressure of the manager threatened to bring on apoplexy, somebody had the gumption to ring down the curtain.

Now, was the band out of a job? That question loomed up ominously in the mind of each of the boys. Lawrence himself didn't even think of it. (He might have saved himself most of the $2200 had he been ousted.) Something else was on his mind. He says: "I felt sorry for the guy who owned the dog."

With such sensibilities Lawrence acted as only he of all the world would act. "Our hero" bearded his enraged boss with the proposition that the dog be given a second chance the next show.

No doubt the man was so taken by surprise, hearing that request, that he scarcely knew what he replied. He agreed to the "second chance." This time the act was not a complete debacle; it was just a mild flop, which did nothing to enhance the band's prestige—or, come to think of it, the dog's.

Now, throughout that second performance, as well as throughout the first, there sat, in one of the front seats, a

little old lady. Nobody could fail to notice her. At the opening show there were scarcely fifty people in the theater,
which could have held many hundreds, so the musicians
were conscious of each separate person in the audience.
That made this poor soul so much the more disconcerting
when all through the show, she sadly shook her head, and
clacked her tongue in disapproval.

"It gets you down," the boys said to one another that
night.

But what was their amazement when she showed up
again for the third performance, and the fourth, and the
fifth, and . . . and . . . So far she wasn't missing a single
performance!

Though with each day the crowd had grown, there was
no forgetting the elderly Calamity Jane, for she never
ceased making disparaging motions and noises.

Four shows a day, two matinees and two evening shows,
it went on! In one week that would mean twenty-eight
shows!

But long before the band had played that often, nerves
began fraying. In fact, about midway through the week,
one of the boys came to Lawrence and said: "I'm quitting.
I have to. I can't stand that woman one more time. She's
driving me nuts."

Lawrence tried to persuade him to reconsider, but had
no success until the manager put in a word: "Oh, you're
talking about old Mrs. X. Don't mind her. She's bats. Her
family don't want to put her in an institution, because she's
harmless, so they give her money to come to all the shows."

After that the boy was able to go along, "smilin'
through."

And there were a few more situations which challenged

Lawrence to do the same. Another quickie engagement of the period took him to a theater in a small Pennsylvania town. Since this particular theater had only one matinee, rather than the customary two, arrangements were made for him to autograph records, during the free time, at the music department of a local furniture store.

On schedule Lawrence entered the department from the bright sunshine outdoors, to see in the dimness a dusty counter and dustier shelves, but at first glance no salesman. Only as his eyes adjusted to the light did he perceive, way in the back of the place, a skinny man, seated in a swivel chair, reading a newspaper. The man didn't greet him, or look up, until Lawrence went over, cleared his throat self-consciously, and mentioned his mission. Then the man grunted: "Uh-huh. Make yourself at home," and reverted to his newspaper.

"I didn't know what to do next," Lawrence says. "I just stood around, leaning first on one foot then the other, waiting for buyers and autograph seekers."

He waited, and waited, and waited.

Finally a woman bustled in like a gust of fresh air, and to Lawrence's joy, she asked for his theme song, "Bubbles in the Wine." Mystery of mysteries! What Welk records did they stock? They didn't have that primary one.

But Lawrence didn't want to lose a sale. Eager-beaver-like, he stepped forward and suggested that he send the record by mail later. Then with his brightest, beamingest smile, he added: "So you like our music?"

"Oh, I don't know," the woman replied. "I haven't heard it. My husband owns the theater where you're playing. We try to keep a file on orchestras we've had there, so that we don't rehire a lemon."

But despite contretemps the Lawrence Welk fortunes very soon took a turn for the better, and Mr. Music Maker found himself going to some of the very best and most charming hotels in Dixie, including the Peabody in Memphis, the Roosevelt in New Orleans, and the Adolphus in Dallas.

By the time he had run through most of them, an important event was due: Fern was expecting another baby. Therefore, instead of feeling elated at his new progress, Lawrence could think of nothing but the old dream of settling down in a home of his own, and ending these eternal tours and one-nighters. He could swing it only if he could find enough long bookings in one locality.

While he chewed the cud of these ideas, his agent, Bill Fredericks, flew to Texas with a sheaf of contracts for Lawrence to sign, contracts which would have taken him over the same ground he had just covered in his Southern route. It was a compliment to his band that he was wanted back so soon for repeat engagements—and at hotels that a few years before Lawrence would have mortgaged anything but his accordion to get into. However, to Bill Fredericks' surprise the bandleader said: "I can't sign those contracts."

"What?" The agent could scarcely believe his ears.

"No," Lawrence insisted. "I can't sign them. We need a home, and I have an idea of how we might get one."

He then proceeded to explain. He had looked over job possibilities, and had steadied his sights on the Trianon Ballroom in Chicago. That large ballroom in the big city was one of the few places that might well provide long bookings, and he hoped . . .

At this point Bill cut in: "But, Lawrence, you can't get

a booking there. I know, because another booking office controls their business."

Lawrence came back: "Bill, I just can't take 'No' that easy."

"That's why you always get what you go after," Bill murmured, while Lawrence went on: "Do you think you're a good enough salesman to get me there for one night? One night is all I ask."

"Wel-l . . ."

At that word Lawrence walked over and shook hands.

"Always I try to get some beginning," he will explain. "I call it getting my foot in the door. It is like the days I'd play for nothing sometimes, hoping it would lead to other things. Usually it did."

This time was no exception. Andrew Karsas, owner of the Trianon, was enough impressed with the band's performance on that one night to offer a contract for six weeks in the near future.

During the interim Lawrence traveled to Dallas, where he had left Fern in her "blessed condition." On the way down he was planning to tell her the happy news of the Trianon contract, and of his hopes of protracting it. When he arrived in Texas, however, the odds are ten to one that he forgot. Fern gave him something more important to talk about. She told him that he was already a father again.

"And it was a boy . . . born on my own birthday, March 11," Lawrence gloats. "He had to be a Junior."

Only one small cloud appeared on his mental horizon: he regretted that his own father had not lived to share this joy with him. But he kept Western Union wires humming, announcing the good tidings to the rest of the family in North Dakota, and to friends throughout the country. He spent thirty-five dollars altogether on telegrams, and he remarks: "At that time I couldn't afford it."

Too bad, with his comparatively new-found voice, that he didn't broadcast it on the air waves. But perhaps he topped that idea. He wrote a song to mark the event. It was entitled "Heaven Is Mine Again," which should reveal his state of mind at the time.

And did he sense that with the birth of his son he was to enter a new phase in his life, a phase in which, for the first time in his career, long engagements in top-notch places would take precedence over one-night stands in small, unknown places?

Actually, though no dramatic clash of cymbals or roll of drums heralded it, Act III of the life of Mr. Music Maker, Lawrence Welk, was beginning. Scene I is laid in Chicago.

To peg the curtain rise on a date: the year was 1940, and the age of the "hero" thirty-seven.

Chapter 24

♫

"My Blue Heaven"

It was all taking shape. The prospect of extended Trianon engagements made possible that desire, cherished long and lovingly by Fern and Lawrence—a permanent home. Always in some vague tomorrow it had hung like a mirage which upon approach dissolved into wispy clouds.

First had come the attempt in Yankton. Lawrence had actually bought a little cottage there, only to have it fade and grow dim, while constant one-night stands took him miles into the hinterland. During two years of ownership he could almost count the evening meals at his own table. Usually at the normal dinner hour Lawrence, on the way to some dance date, would be eating in a diner by the side of the road.

Then he had made that other try for a home in Omaha. He had been optimistic enough to buy the house surrounded with a few acres where supposedly he might putter with chicken farming—and eventually, perhaps, settle down to it in earnest. The place was out from town, west of the suburb called Benson, on Main Street, but to the paterfamilias it remained little more than a mailing address. The mix-up with the Musicians Union, barring him from local jobs, meant "on the road," with no breaks worth mentioning. Fern was left to manage the place, which in Lawrence's absence seemed only a ponderous white elephant.

"These two houses were the nearest thing to our own little nest, like the songs say," declares Lawrence, "and we didn't keep either of them more than a year or two. The rest of the time, it was just rented places, furnished or unfurnished, and often just apartments, hotels, or motels. It got awful monotonous."

Though Fern and the children could not follow Lawrence to every whistle stop, they did make an effort to reflect the broad pattern of his treks. Intermittently on the move, they had to choose a place they could leave on short notice.

If Lawrence had a number of engagements booked ahead in a given area, they would have to pull up stakes and follow along. These gypsy journeyings had already meant a couple of school switches for Shirley, the eldest child, while for both little girls the changes prevented their having the same playmates long enough to make friends.

"Maybe these weren't such big troubles to kids that age," Lawrence concedes, "but they were another straw to help break the camel's back. The worst part was how terrible the life was for Fern."

When she would pile the two children, plus the bulging, battered luggage, into the car, and set off, cross-country if need be, she often did not know where she would find a place to stay en route, or at their destination. One thing only was certain: comfortable rented apartments or houses were not readily available to people with small children.

On one tour Donna avowed: "When I get big, I'm going

to open a place that takes just dogs and kids—no grown-ups."

Lawrence didn't worry so much about dogs. He says: "There are folks who will welcome dog or cat owners but who will not rent to couples with children. That's not right. Those same folks may talk big words about security, but don't they know that we can't have security—not any of us in this country—unless we look after the family. The family is the first thing."

When at last they would find a place to hang their hats, the brunt of whatever inconveniences it possessed fell on Fern. "If I went on a short hop," Lawrence explains, "Fern would stay with the children. Most of the time she had to be the man as well as the lady of the house."

But even without extra inconveniences that double role would have taxed her strength, emotionally and physically. About the latter Shirley attests: "Mother was the one who had to wrestle with storm windows, screens, blown-out fuses, stopped-up drains, and all that."

And about the emotional factor Lawrence himself drops some hints. He makes clear that when two people are in love, it is "terrible hard" to be apart so much, and he lets slip that his "good wife" wanted "a home together," and that she, as he did, felt that something was lacking in those first years of marriage.

Now, since Chicago looked like the Promised Land of lengthy job opportunity, the time had come for another try at home establishment.

From their apartment in the area they undertook house-hunting expeditions. At first, however, they ran into a few snags, but Lawrence points out: "Better later than never.

In 1942, I put a down payment on a place. It was in the River Forest section."

Home, sweet home! Every time Lawrence walked in the front door, he marveled afresh that this was his—all his. And Fern never had an instant's doubt about the exact moment he did walk in, since he would flip on the radio, or begin humming a tune, just from the sheer joy of finding himself within the walls of his "blue heaven."

For nine full years, until 1951, that is, the Welks continued to live there ensemble. The children put down roots. Shirley went to grammar school, then to Trinity High, where she stayed the whole four years, long enough to make real friends, and finally she went on with some of them to matriculate at Marquette University. Donna began at St. Vincent Ferrer's Parochial School, and stayed there throughout the entire eight years, while little Larry started his schooling there and had no breaks either, until the big California move. With a grin Lawrence sums up: "It was real wonderful."

All this was possible, be it repeated, because the Music Maker was able to sign up year after year for "long" engagements in the area. In the music business "long" is usually defined as six or eight weeks.

Besides the Trianon Ballroom he often found local jobs at the Chicago and Oriental theatres, and at the Aragon Ballroom (not to be confused with the Aragon in Southern California), under the same management as the Trianon.

Comments Lawrence: "This was a new life—and better than all those one-night stands that we'd had for mostly fifteen years before. And now we had new prestige, too. The Trianon was known to hire only top-notch bands, so visitors to Chicago, as well as folks who lived there, would come to the place. They went home and spread the name of our band. Our broadcasts from the Trianon over WGN helped us an awful lot too. Suddenly we had a real national reputation."

Yet between Chicago engagements Lawrence still traveled. When he had to travel in the fall or winter, the family no longer attempted to follow. Only during the summer vacation months did they revert to the vagabond life. "Fern was glad that she didn't have to change the kids' schools," says Lawrence.

So much did summertime and tour time continue to be synonymous that one season, for example, Lawrence played in thirty-eight ballrooms in eight states, Minnesota, South Dakota, Indiana, Iowa, Michigan, Nebraska, Ohio, and Illinois.

"It was scads of fun," says young Larry today. "I liked summers better'n any other time."

But did his mother and sisters agree with him? Shirley shows a certain lack of enthusiasm when she describes some of their trips. "You know Daddy—the darling would get us anything in the world we wanted, but one part of him lives a dreamy kind of existence. He never even notices physical comfort. Often when we'd stop for the night in some country town, he'd get out of the car and go up to the proprietor of a tourist house and say: 'I have my wife and three children with me. Can you fix us up for the night?' But he would forget to mention a private bath, or to inquire about what kind of accommodations were available. I remember a time, just before we moved to California. Daddy pulled his usual line about 'my wife and three children' at this tourist home, but he didn't make clear that one 'child,' me, was then almost twenty years old, and that even the youngest child was a big, overgrown boy of eleven or twelve. When we got inside, wilted and weary after driving all day, we found that all they had for us 'children' were cribs. How Donna and I jackknifed ourselves into a crib I'll never know. Larry didn't try. He slept on the sofa."

Then she tells of the time they were traveling through the Dakotas, headed for an Indian reservation where Lawrence was to play. They stopped at night at a string of adobe huts calling itself a motel. They entered, to find that the whole family was expected to sleep in one room, on beds lined up only inches apart.

That was the least of their troubles!

Facilities were strictly primitive. If a patron wanted to wash, he would have to resort to the well.

Lawrence left for his playing date, and Fern sent her Jack and Jill, Larry and Donna, to fetch a pail of water. They brought it back dutifully, and Larry couldn't at first understand why his mother was shocked to see him washing from it. "He didn't know," Shirley explains, "that you're supposed to pour just some of the water at a time into a washbowl, so that each person can have fresh water when his turn comes."

Finally they retired. According to Shirley's story: "The beds were rickety, the mattresses were thin pads stuffed with straw, and the pillows . . . well, the first thing Donna said when she put her head down was: 'Mother, my pillow smells.' It did, too. They all did. They were musty. Every few minutes she'd make some comment about her pillow, till Mother told her not to say another thing that night."

Scarcely had the family quieted down when they were disturbed by voices outside. Lawrence had come back to the "motel" and tried the door of the adjacent, identical

hut. He found it locked, so he called: "Honey, let me in."
No response.

"Hey, honey! Honey, let me in. This is Lawrence."

A pause, and then a bass voice boomed: "Don't you
honey me again, or I'll bust you in the jaw."

Finally, grasping the facts, Fern jumped from bed, and
ran to her door. "Lawrence," she stage-whispered, "you
have the wrong place. Here we are."

Inside, Lawrence lost no time undressing and getting to
bed. His first words when his head hit the pillow: "Honey,
you know, this pillow smells."

He was baffled when his remark evoked laughter.

Again the family quieted down, but nobody could sleep.
Shirley recounts: "One or the other of us would keep rear-
ing up in bed and look across the room to find several pairs
of wide-open eyes staring back. Finally Daddy proposed:
'Let's get up and drive on to the next stop.'"

It was 4:30. Yet driving at such an hour was no novelty
to the Welks. Often on a tour, in order to save time primarily, and money secondarily, they would engage sleeping accommodations only alternate nights. For instance,
they would drive all day, arriving at about dinnertime in
the town where Lawrence was to play. After dinner Lawrence would go to his ballroom, and Fern and the children
would go to a movie and then return to the car to sleep as
best they could for a few hours. After the dance Lawrence
would join them and they would drive on. At the next destination they would go to a motel or hotel and, if the hour
were still early enough, nap before dinner.

Strenuous? No doubt about that, but Fern kept reminding herself of the favorable aspects of the Chicago setup:
it supplied so many jobs in the vicinity that at least Law-

At a teen-age dance in the Aragon Ballroom, Ocean Park, Calif., Donna leads the orchestra while Lawrence Welk and Alice Lon look on.

Champagne Lady Alice Lon and Lawrence Welk.

Lawrence Welk leading his orchestra at Blimp Hangar, Santa Ana, Calif., in 1954, before an audience of 51,000 people.

At a Fan Club picnic Lawrence Welk plays chef, handing a plate he has just filled to one of his fans, Mrs. Margaret Robinson.

Lawrence Welk with the Lennon Sisters—Peggy, Janet, Diane, and Kathy.

Lawrence Welk, 1957.

rence's winter traveling was much less than in former days. And when a winter tour did whisk him away from the windy city, the family knew that he would be returning in a matter of days, weeks, or months to the sure harbor of the Trianon, and the house in River Forest.

Of his home-comings the children say: "We kids always loved seeing Daddy get back after a trip. He's fun to have around. And besides that it was like a party. Mom killed the fatted calf for him—you know the best china, flowers on the table, scrumptious food and all. We grew up thinking Daddy was a sort of king we really should be on our best behavior for—but a jolly, wonderful king, who teased us, and loved us, and, I guess, spoiled us a little."

As for Lawrence himself, he found it an unfailing comfort to be able to return always to the familiar spot, and to "Fern and the kids," his sure refuge and balance in a giddy world. Clearly the woman whom Shirley called "a genius in the home" kept ready and waiting for him the kind of peaceful, warm haven that all men ideally envision at the end of a long road.

But if Lawrence was happy to come home, he still cherished the hope of someday making an Eastern tour which would culminate in a New York performance. That dream had lived in his imagination for more years than he bothered to count.

In 1943 the bid came from the big city.

He set off for this particular Treasure Island with great expectations, but he confesses succinctly: "It wasn't exactly like my dreams."

The band was neither a smash hit nor a dismal failure. It drew a good enough following, and some papers carried moderately favorable reviews.

So much and nothing more!

They played at the Capitol Theatre on Broadway, and Lawrence could not do his best in such a place. On the huge, remote bandstand, lifted above and cut off from the "folks," he looked out into the cavernous immensity and found that he could not even see the faces of his audience. The homey Welk technique was lost in space. It was like dropping a daisy into the Grand Canyon and waiting for the crash.

Incidentally Ralph Edwards, who now produces the TV show *This Is Your Life,* and who in March 1957 featured among his guests one Lawrence Welk, was billed on the Capitol Theatre program at the same time the Music Maker was.

Meanwhile, from New York it was back to Chicago for the band.

In Chicago the Welks, for almost the first time in their married life, managed a little social life. It was the first time they had stayed in one place long enough for much of that sort of thing. Among their group of friends were the Spauldings. Lawrence could say gratefully: "When I'm away, I can always count on good folks, like the Spauldings, to give Fern helpful hands, if she needs anything. That makes me easy in my mind."

Today Lawrence employs Ed Spaulding in California as a business administrator and personal trouble-shooter.

"It is characteristic of Lawrence," remarks Ed, "that he never forgets a friend."

But how could Lawrence forget the Spauldings? Unintentionally, and indirectly, they were the cause of Lawrence almost losing his wife.

♫

Chapter 25

"Keep the Home Fires Burning"

It was Lawrence's birthday, March 11, 1945. He wasn't home to celebrate it with his family, but was playing in New Orleans. The engagement, a routine thing, presented no special problems, so Lawrence was relaxed. Says he: "I didn't know what was going to happen."

Meanwhile, in Chicago, Fern sat home with the children, feeling perhaps a bit blue that Lawrence was away on such an important occasion. If she tried to picture him in the Southern city, where undoubtedly the weather at that date was balmy and springlike, she would have found it hard to do, for March 11 of 1945 in Chicago was cold and rainy.

But whatever her musings, they were interrupted by the phone ringing. It was the Spauldings. They suggested that they come by and take her out for the evening.

Why not? She accepted thankfully, and a little later, as her friends drew up before the house, she hurried out, throwing a kiss to the children.

She did not return for weeks.

In the course of that evening, driving along the slippery streets, a car emerged at a certain intersection and hit the Spaulding car broadside. Its three occupants were all sitting in the front seat—Ed at the wheel, Mrs. Spaulding in the center, and Fern on the right end. The car hit on the right.

Although what immediately followed is vague in Fern's memory, she is under the impression that she never completely lost consciousness. Anyhow, by the time the ambulance arrived, she was alert enough to realize that she could not move her legs. She was paralyzed from the waist down.

Because the Spauldings both "looked dreadful" to her, she wrongly assumed that they were worse off than herself, and she proposed that they be placed on stretchers, saying: "I'm able to sit up."

Sit up she did, all the way to the hospital. Once there, she begged for a phone. She was told that someone in an official capacity had notified Lawrence, but she still insisted that she wanted the phone. At least she could talk personally to her children, so that they wouldn't be any more frightened than need be.

"I'm OK," she told Shirley, "but hospital authorities are cautious. They'll keep me for tests and all. Now, there's one thing I want you to be sure to do: sleep in my bed because your little brother always comes in my room in the morning, and he'll be upset if he finds the bed empty. Do everything as usual. You can manage . . . but call Jayne Walton in the morning."

Nurses then carried Fern off, and almost immediately she went into a state of shock. For some days thereafter she talked to no one coherently. Her condition was certainly very grave, if not critical.

Her pelvis had multiple fractures, her sacroiliac was sprained, and her left hipbone broken.

When Lawrence reached Chicago, he was told by the doctors that there was doubt whether his wife would ever walk again.

Meanwhile, before he arrived in town, Jayne Walton, who, after six years as Champagne Lady, had recently given up that job to get married, rushed to the Welk home to take care of the children. It was a strange interval. The children, when they speak of it today, mention Cream of Wheat. It was a symbol.

Having been told that Cream of Wheat was the usual breakfast fare, Jayne proceeded to cook it for the first morning meal she prepared. She had never tackled the stuff before, and she tried very hard.

Donna, however, just sat there with tears dripping into it.

"Eat your breakfast, darling," Jayne urged.

"Mother's Cream of Wheat doesn't have lumps like this," Donna sobbed.

"Uh-uh, it doesn't," echoed Larry, and began to wail too.

Poor Jayne's stricken face would have been enough to stimulate Shirley's tear ducts if they hadn't already been in full production out of sympathy for Donna and Larry; she knew that they were crying, not because of lumpy cereal, but because they missed their mother and were frightened.

Then Larry asked: "Will my mom die?" and Jayne's eyes overflowed too.

Not a soul touched breakfast that morning.

But Jayne did cook the children other and more satisfactory meals, until a few days later, upon the arrival of Cornelia Weber, she returned to her own home.

Cornelia was a cousin whom Lawrence asked to come stay with the children and "to keep the home fires up."

Apparently Lawrence was able to plan well enough to make provision for the children, and to go on automatically with the music business, but in some respects he suffered a state of shock analogous to Fern's. He was half dazed by what had happened.

It seemed strange beyond believing that his "good wife," this efficient, energetic, woman, should be invalided. And he simply could not grasp the idea that she might not walk again. He says: "I didn't know what to make of things. I just prayed harder than ever."

When Fern returned from the hospital, her cheerful courage convinced him that everything would be all right again—pretty soon. And the children took their cue from the adults. Here was an unpleasant fantasy that would pass in due time. Meanwhile, they would pray, and try to be patient.

Actually after some weeks Fern was able to sit up and dangle her legs over the side of the bed; then she ventured to stand; later she demanded crutches and taught herself to get around; finally she really was "all right again," and one day, climbing into her car, she drove herself to the hospital to return the crutches. Today she hasn't even a limp to remind her of her ordeal.

All the while, she had encouraged Lawrence to maintain his usual schedule. World War II was still in progress, and he was receiving more dance bids than he could handle, particularly since for the last few years he had set aside some part of each week to play gratis for the armed forces.

"It was the least I could do," he explains. "I'm an American, and I hope a strong kind. I heard enough of the 'old country' from my parents to know that only in the United States, where business doesn't have all kinds of government restrictions, can a man begin with nothing, and just by working hard, go ahead as far as he wants. As long as we keep our free system, the only thing that can hold a man back will be himself."

In the course of his numerous army performances Lawrence met Sam Lutz, the man who plays a supporting role in the Lawrence Welk drama today. Sam was in the Army —a sergeant in Special Services—and it was his job to find weekly entertainment for the GI's at Gardiner General Hospital.

"Show business is erratic," he says. "Seems like I was always being stuck without a performer. When I was in a jam, I could send an SOS to Lawrence Welk. He was the most obliging fellow in the world."

A few years later Sam, having received his discharge, went to the West Coast with the hope of forming a theatrical agency there. Lawrence was playing at the Aragon, in Southern California, and it didn't take long for Sam and him to get together to talk "old times."

Just then Lawrence retained a huge, impersonal agency, so he was not averse to switching his business to Sam and a nascent company, where a client could count on plenty of attention. Also Lawrence adds: "Sam was an old friend. I was glad to be able to help him get started."

Lawrence Welk was Sam Lutz's first client.

A few months later the firm of Gabbe, Lutz and Heller was formed, and today it handles the orchestra's business from handsome offices at Hollywood and Vine, above the famed Brown Derby restaurant. From the same eyrie the agency also handles Liberace and other glittering personalities.

Speaking of the bandleader back in Chicago, Sam avows: "Lawrence was different from a good many entertainers I dealt with. None of them received money, of course, but lots of them would expect little concessions and favors. I remember one gal. She said sure she'd do this army hospital show, if I'd see to it that she was slipped a couple dozen boxes of facial tissues. Paper products were hard to buy during the war. Well, I couldn't get the facial tissues for her, so, believe it or not, she refused to play for the hospital. Lawrence was never like that."

In four years Lawrence supplied more shows for Chicago's Gardiner General Hospital than any other entertainer. Also he played for a number of army camps too during those years (and even after peace was declared).

Besides that he became a crack salesman of war bonds. He didn't make any announcement about them from the bandstand; he feared his German accent would prevent rather than promote sales, but he and the boys would sell war stamps in person to their patrons. Lawrence called his group the Bomber Brigade, since their object was to raise sufficient funds to defray construction costs of a bomber.

Also he did his "bit" to "keep the home fires" of justice burning brightly in his native land, and there must be told a little by-plot, which thickened the general over-all plot of Lawrence's life at this time. It concerns Mrs. A, an old friend of Fern's, and it involves a crime. Mrs. A, while working at a large institution, had been blamed for the disappearance of a considerable sum of the institution's funds.

Fern was appalled. She knew the girl well enough to feel sure that Mrs. A was innocent. What was up?

At Fern's urging Lawrence flew to the scene of the crime and began a one-man investigation. The more deeply he delved into the mess, the more convinced he became that Mrs. A's friends must be right when they said she was "framed."

Meantime the girl was arrested, convicted, and sent to prison. That really galvanized Fern and Lawrence into action. They became a regular Mr. and Mrs. North working on a case.

First of all, Lawrence, who ordinarily abhorred debt, raised money by using his house as security, and then he put up a bond for Mrs. A. Next he visited lawyers, asking them to re-examine the evidence.

Because his tours did not frequently take him into the city where he could confer with these lawyers, he had to find time and means to travel back and forth to that city. To cut transportation costs, he secured engagements to play for army camps in the locality, so that he could have more opportunity to work nearby.

Fern also was busy. She wrote to practically everybody who had ever known Mrs. A and asked for their opinion of the girl. She and Lawrence collected stacks of letters testifying to Mrs. A's upright character. Finally, through the instrumentality of Lancelot and his "good wife," the Parole Board reviewed the case, and they released the girl at the earliest moment the law allowed, one year after her incarceration.

♫

Chapter 26

"East Side, West Side"

While Chicago was good to Lawrence, it is not to be confused with Utopia. "There were," as he puts it, "some flies stuck in the ointment."

One thing Fern particularly disliked was the long distance Lawrence had to travel back and forth between home and the Trianon. The twenty-one-mile drive, mostly through traffic, took a full hour each way. "Many a time, I'd worry myself half sick," she admits. "Lawrence would get so sleepy, driving home at 3 A.M., that he would have to pull over to the side of the road and nap a bit before he could go on. I was afraid that one night he might not pull over in time, and would fall asleep at the wheel. Then I could just see the car careening across the highway, to crash into a tree or something."

Of course the Welks might have moved closer to the Trianon if that had been feasible, but in the vicinity of the ballroom there was no residential area. Moreover distance was only one irksome detail. Lawrence himself accumulated a few small grievances.

He mentions occasional differences of opinion with the Trianon owner, Karzas. For instance, Mr. Karzas had been upset when Lawrence had tried to vary Champagne Music and go in for "class." Explosively he had threatened: "Get back in the groove or you're fired. We're losing customers."

Says Lawrence candidly: "Karzas was right about this. Folks couldn't dance as well to the modern arrangements. Champagne Music put the girl back in the boy's arms—where she belongs."

But was Karzas's excitable temperament a bit hard on Lawrence's nerves?

The bandleader doesn't say so. He speaks of another objection to the Chicago setup. The ballroom operators in the city knew that he preferred to play in the immediate area, where he could be with his family, so, taking advantage of that, they tended to offer him considerably less money than he was paid when he went on tour. "The difference seemed too much," says Lawrence, "and besides I felt that everything combined was getting me stuck in a kind of rut, where I couldn't ever get any bigger."

Of course, if he wanted only monetary advancement, he could achieve it simply by traveling more frequently, but the hardships and hazards of traveling were such that he would have liked to reduce, not increase, traveling. In fact one particular experience of the era almost made him resolve never to budge from his own back yard again.

Going from Denver to Salt Lake City, the troupe was caught in a blizzard in Utah. The road was lost in a white blur and they were winding their way over a steep mountain pass. Only inch by inch could they creep forward, guessing by the line of trees the road's edge and the brink of the incline. Finally they overtook a truck, and from then on could follow in its tracks, as it too proceeded with the nerve-racking uncertainty which had marked their previous progress.

When they reached their destination after driving all day and all night, they were as exhausted physically and emotionally as if they had crawled on all fours through a hail of bullets. The drummer was running a 103° temperature, induced by the ordeal. No wonder that Lawrence did not consider additional travel the answer to his situation.

While he was still groping for whatever *was* the right answer, he received a bid to play on the West Coast. In 1945, at Dan London's invitation, Lawrence and the band went to San Francisco's St. Francis Hotel, for a six-week engagement. Those six weeks stretched into six months— testimony enough that Mr. Music Maker was well received in the city of the Golden Gate.

From there he went to Southern California, to the Aragon Ballroom in Ocean Park. Again he was booked for six weeks, and this six weeks became seven months, thus making his Western stay, that time, total thirteen months.

During the period, Lawrence flew East for no engagements whatever, but only for the purpose of seeing his family, and they flew West several times to see him.

"It's funny that the Aragon turned out the way it did," says Lawrence. "When I first saw the place, it didn't look good to me. I didn't think our band fitted in there."

But how did he happen to stay as long as seven months that time? Usually ballrooms change bands much more frequently. Lawrence has an explanation: " 'Pops' Gordon —that is Gordon Sadrup—wanted something to stand up against the real strong competition of the Casino Ballroom, which is in Ocean Park too, just about a block away from the Aragon. The operators there always hired the biggest names in the country, and they had a couple of

extra-special ones as coming attractions. Pops asked my
advice about what band he should get after my six weeks
were up. I suggested Guy Lombardo, but Pops said that he
had already asked Guy and couldn't get him. I mentioned
some other bands, like Jan Garber's, but it ended with Pops
offering me the job. I was bowled all over. I had never
played against the kind of competition I saw ahead, and I
told Pops that. He said I could do it, so, kind of scared, I
agreed to try. It was worth the effort, and the chance.
Maybe competition is good for you—makes you do your
best. And for the first time in my life, I felt that I was in
the big time for sure."

Perhaps being "in the big time" led to Lawrence's invitation to the Roosevelt Hotel in New York. At any rate,
that was the next important steppingstone in the Music
Maker's career. In 1947 he went there for a spring fill-in
booking.

For twenty years Guy Lombardo had held sway at the
Roosevelt, and Lawrence, who as he avows "thought a lot
of this bandleader," wanted to play the game of follow-
the-leader. Quite simply, then, he asked Guy's advice:
"What can I do to make the folks back here like us?"

Mr. Lombardo was very generous. Declares Lawrence:
"He helped us a lot, especially with advice about songs
and tempos."

So it is not without reason that Lawrence Welk was,
and still is, often called the second Guy Lombardo.

One night a woman approached Lawrence and said: "I
came all the way from Canada to hear you in person. I
love your music, and I'm proud that you're a Canadian
too."

"But I'm not a Canadian," Lawrence answered. "I'm an American, born in North Dakota."

"North Dakota!" echoed his vis-à-vis. "Why, everybody up our way thinks you're Canadian."

"Are you sure that you haven't got me mixed up with Guy Lom—"

"Oh . . . aren't you Guy Lombardo?" gasped the woman.

A reasonable facsimile, all right!

But there are many who say that the second Lombardo has outstripped the first, that the protégé has surpassed the tutor. However, Lawrence himself is not one of them. He says: "I could never take the place of Guy Lombardo."

At any rate, Lawrence did "please the folks" who flocked to the Roosevelt, and for three successive seasons he was called to New York for repeat engagements.

But before going on with that, Lawrence has a little story to tell about what happened on his way to the first Roosevelt engagement. As usual, he ran in a number of one-nighters en route. In Iowa his Champagne Lady, Joan Mowery, became ill and had to fly home for an operation. Lawrence phoned Joe Kayser in Chicago, and asked him to send a substitute for Joan—and pronto, please!

In short order the girl arrived. She was a long, tall, dangling creature, not much to look at, but oh so willing and determined to make good.

Lawrence had his misgivings the minute he saw her, but at least she deserved a chance. He heard her sing. It was then that his misgivings were tripled.

"I didn't see how I could use her," he says, "but with her so anxious for the job, it was awful hard to turn her down. I tried to say it real easy and kind, but even so when I started talking to her, the tears just rushed out, and she carried on something awful."

"Oh, Mr. Welk, you can't do this to me," she sobbed. "My big chance! And I've told all my friends back home, and . . . Oh, Mr. Welk, I'll do anything, but please, please, please don't send me home."

It was too much for Lawrence to withstand. He softened. And he says: "We rehearsed extra carefully."

Carefully indeed! The girl asked Lawrence about every gesture she should make, so that she might perform down to the last hairsbreadth as he wanted.

She was to sing a duet with one of the boys, featuring the song "Doin What Comes Naturlly." In the course of it the boy was supposed to put his arm around her, and she was to look at him warningly. Next, he was supposed to lean toward her as though to kiss her, then she was to spurn him with a gesture and whirl gracefully away from him. They practiced the routine under Lawrence's observant supervision, and apparently tall Tillie had it pat.

Evening came. The crowd arrived. Now the song! The pair began it, the boy at the proper cue put his arm around the girl, she scowled at him, he attempted the kiss, and then—shades of Mack Sennett!—it happened. She gave him a blow with all the fervor of her desire to obey instructions and "spurn," and what did she do but knock the fellow down. Suddenly he lay sprawling in the center of the stage.

For a moment there was stunned silence. Even the orchestra had faltered in amazement. Then the boy, struggling to his feet, shattered the stillness with a disgusted: "I quit."

As though those two words were a signal, the orchestra

to a man dissolved in laughter. It was all Lawrence himself could do to grab his accordion and stagger to the middle of the bandstand for a number.

"As I looked out over the upturned faces of the audience, I could tell by the expressions that folks didn't know whether all this was a cooked-up gag, or an accident," he says.

And he didn't enlighten them.

In retrospect Lawrence sees that amusing incidents were a regular monthly, or even weekly, supplement to all his touring days. He tells of the time, some years before, when the Champagne Music Makers were covering the same familiar Midwest territory. They had finished playing for a dance at Tom Archer's Tromar Ballroom in Des Moines at 1 A.M. Then, having stopped by a diner for a sandwich, they set out on their travels, intending to drive all night until they reached Norfolk, Nebraska, and King's Ballroom, where they were to play the next engagement.

Toward 5 A.M. everybody began to feel very weary, wilted, and woebegone. The Champagne Lady, Jayne Walton, particularly wanted nothing so much as a hot bath and a place to sleep. She put her head back against the car cushions and tried to nap, but Lawrence was talking: "See that farmhouse over there?" (He indicated a place up the road a bit.) "A good friend of mine lives in it."

"I wish you'd pipe down and let a girl sleep," Jayne mumbled. "Besides you're probably just boasting. Everybody's your friend."

"What's his name?" one of the boys teased.

"Bet you don't know him at all," the girl took up.

"That's where you're wrong," retorted Lawrence, and

then in a bantering tone matching theirs he added: "Let's stop and see him."

He turned into the farmer's driveway and hailed a man going to the barn to milk the cows: "Hi, Harry!"

"Why, Lawrence!" came the reply. "Where did you come from? You must stay to breakfast."

The crowd piled out of the car for breakfast—all but Lawrence. He said he'd go into town for Sunday church and then join them a little later.

"Jayne, she was a good scout, but even so, she never forgave me for dumping her there." Lawrence chuckles as he tells about that day. "First she asked where the bathroom was, but of course Harry didn't have any city bathroom. He—or I guess it was his wife—told Jayne to go out behind the barn and she'd see . . . Well, she didn't like what she did see."

However, being stranded, Jayne and the boys rested for a while, and later in the day nothing would satisfy their genial host but that they stay for a midday dinner.

By that time, of course, Lawrence had returned to join them for a sumptuous meal.

"It was grand," he reminisces, "two kinds of meat, sweet potatoes, white potatoes, hot biscuits . . . I can't tell what all."

Grand? Well, yes . . . except for a slight flaw. A breeze was blowing that afternoon, from the direction of the pigsty: it blew straight into the dining room, and into the nostrils of the diners. Poor Jayne! She wasn't a country lass, and with each breath she drew she turned a shade greener. Finally, she just had to excuse herself and go outdoors. By this time her complexion was a perfect match for the grass.

When the troupe drove off late that afternoon, Jayne's first and only comment was: "No more farms or I'm through."

Incidentally, she could have meant exactly what she said, for Welk personnel are not bound by the legal strings of a contract. After giving two weeks' notice required by union rules, anyone, or all of the band, could walk off the job.

That there is very little job turnover must be due to one cause only: people like working for Lawrence Welk.

But why no contracts? Contracts are considered as much a part of show business as make-up.

Lawrence has his reasons: "I'd rather have folks working for me because they want to than because they have to. They do better work then. Where I come from, a handshake is as good as a written contract any day."

With all business associates Lawrence dodges contracts when he can. "If a person is going to be dishonest," he says, "there's always a way he can find to wriggle out of a contract. If he is honest, I don't need one."

Honesty, one of Lawrence's pet subjects, usually prompts a Welkese dissertation. "It is so foolish not to be honest," Lawrence avers. "If I see a fellow trying to chisel a few dollars here or there, I may let him take those dollars, but in the end I'll probably have to fire him from a job paying fifteen or twenty thousand a year maybe."

"Honesty is best policy." Is that what he's saying? Not exactly, for he adds: "But you shouldn't be honest for gain. If you act good because you think it will make you money, then you're not really good, and people sense that and won't trust you when the heat's on. It's like when somebody is nice to you for what he can get from you.

You soon see through that, and you think less of him than if he had never been nice to you in the first place."

So Lawrence talks. But enough of talk for the moment. What did Lawrence do about his Chicago situation? Why didn't he or couldn't he find a niche for himself on either the East or the West Coast? That's what he would have liked at this time.

♫

Chapter 27

"More and More"

Lawrence grew more and more restless. Each time he returned to Chicago from a long tour or engagement, he saw the situation in the home town through darker glasses.

But at one point he thought he would be able to leave it all behind him. He had gone off to an engagement at the Statler in Buffalo in mid-December. In keeping with the season he had prepared a show featuring special Christmas songs and music. Because of the sacred nature of some of the songs he asked the crowd not to applaud until the conclusion of the forty-five-minute program. Usually, when the applause did come, it was tremendous and prolonged. One night while it was still going on, a well-dressed middle-aged man, together with his diamond-bedecked wife, approached Lawrence on the bandstand and asked: "Could I have a word with you?"

As the Music Maker bent his head to listen, the stranger complimented the leader at great length on the band's performance and then ended up with a proposition: "My best friend is owner of the Statler chain. Would you like to play his hotels for the next couple of years? You could begin at the Statler in Washington, go to New York, and so on. I can arrange it, but first I'd like to know—would it interest you?"

It definitely would and did interest Lawrence, and he was about to say so most enthusiastically when the wife, who had seemed edgy all along, plucked her husband's sleeve. "Come on, Charlie," she urged. "Let's go." Then, turning to Lawrence, she winked and said: "Don't pay any attention to my husband. We've just come from a cocktail party."

Enough said?

Anyway, with that the two departed, leaving Lawrence to ponder the irony of the gods of show business.

But during this somewhat unsatisfactory latter part of the Chicago era, there was one large boost of the Lawrence Welk career. The maestro gives Leo Fortin, his trumpet man at that time, credit for the idea.

Lawrence was traveling along the highway with Leo on a tour, when a billboard sign caught the attention of both men. It was advertising Miller High-Life beer, "the champagne of bottled beer." Leo remarked: "I have a friend who knows Roy Bernier, the advertising manager of Miller Brewing Company. I understand that the company is going to expand its advertising, Lawrence, why don't you run up to Milwaukee to see them, tell them you can advertise their product by tying in the champagne of beer with the champagne of music?"

Without hesitation Lawrence answered: "I'll do that. It's a real wonderful idea! And if I get busy, and keep putting it off, just you keep reminding me."

Actually he didn't put it off long. He made that Milwaukee trip, met Mr. Bernier, who introduced him to "that grand gentleman" Fred Miller.* The rest followed quickly. Sponsored by Miller High-Life beer, Lawrence Welk went on his first nationwide broadcast. It was on the ABC network.

The program was reasonably successful. Moreover, the voice of radio carrying across the land brought its echo of prestige and acclamation everywhere, not to speak of more and more dance jobs, here, there and yonder. Fred Miller, believing in personal appearances for the band, as a means of putting over the radio program, had made them a part of his deal with Lawrence. Touring, it seems, is an inevitable part of the bandleader's life.

On many a highway could be seen a little caravan of cars, bright-hued with a decal of the familiar Miller High-Life advertisement of the girl sitting jauntily on a crescent moon, while the lettering (or some of it) spelled out "The Champagne Music of Lawrence Welk."

One of the tours took them to the Northwest. It was a memorable tour, not because it is a clue to the Lawrence Welk success story, but because it reveals a facet of Lawrence Welk the man.

He felt that some of the boys had the wrong attitude. They didn't want to practice; they didn't want to work. They were just looking for a soft job. "Especially with this real wonderful opportunity with Miller, that made me see some red," Lawrence comments, "though I can always blow off the handle when I meet laziness, or this dishonesty of expecting something for nothing. I need more patience."

Shirley would disagree with her father's statement about requiring patience. In fact, she declares: "If I had

* Fred Miller was killed in a plane accident in 1955.

to name Daddy's one outstanding characteristic, it would be patience. He bears with a person for ages and ages, giving whoever it is every possible chance. People figure lots of times that they're getting away with something, that gullible, naïve Daddy doesn't even see what they're doing right under his nose. He sees all right, and he understands. It's his patience that makes him hold off for so long. It's only when he decides that the case is hopeless, and when he figures that no amount of time is going to change the person or persons involved, that he at long last lowers the boom. And are people surprised!"

When Lawrence "lowered the boom," he broke up a rehearsal by declaring that the whole band to a man was fired. "I was ready," he avers, "to go out and find musicians who were willing to give fair work for fair wages."

However, as soon as the boys had absorbed the shock of their dismissal, they decided that they would be more than willing to practice adequately, and to work in all ways on Lawrence Welk's terms, if he would reinstate them in their jobs. One by one, they sidled into his room and said this in their own words.

"I rehired most of them," he says, "but only after I made sure that their attitude had changed, and that their promises of turning a different leaf were sincere."

When he went on tour again, he felt that the band was behind him, willing to do their best. This next tour through the Midwest was sheer routine except for one notable event. In St. Louis the maestro happened to hear an accordionist named Myron Floren, playing in a little Western-type band. "The fellow is good," Lawrence exclaimed, and forthwith offered him a job.

Returning to Chicago with his new find, he ran into

Karzas's opposition. The manager protested: "You can't do that, Lawrence. The patrons say that this new fellow is better than you are. You'll have to get rid of him—quick."

"Of course he's better than I am," Lawrence answered blandly. "That's why I hired him. The only kind of musicians I do hire are fellows better than I am."

"Are you crazy, man!" the manager bellowed. "Would Dorsey sign a trombone player better than he is? What kind of showmanship would you call that?"

"The best," Lawrence replied. "The best showmanship is to give folks the finest thing you can get. Myron stays."

Baffled, Karzas shook his head, but he didn't argue further.

"When Lawrence is sure he's right about something," says one of the boys, "you can't any more argue him out of it than you can talk a traffic cop out of handing you a ticket."

The band, improved by the addition to its personnel, was as popular as ever at the Trianon. With no spectacular offer coming from either coast, it looked, as Fern says, "like Lawrence would be there till we were both gray and grumpy."

Well, why not relax and enjoy the situation he had? Theoretically Lawrence might agree that that was wise; the trouble was that he is not the relaxing sort.

He realized that he was not badly off, that in fact he had reached the top echelons of his profession in most respects, yet another thought obtruded: music was a precarious business. To a large extent it depended upon the whims of a public, allegedly fickle. The cautious man should have an ace in the hole, so Lawrence concluded: "I got the idea again that I'd work up some commercial deal on the side. The day might come when I'd have to, as well as want to, stop touring altogether. Then I could spend my time on my new enterprise, and with Fern and the kids."

His thoughts turned toward "the food business." He and Fern (the latter a veritable culinary expert despite the fact that before marriage she told Lawrence she couldn't cook) experimented with recipes in their own kitchen, and concocted a special sauce for hamburgers, re-named by Lawrence "squeezeburgers."

A squeezeburger was to be served on a rhythm roll with piccolo pickles and fiddlestick fries, and packaged in an accordion-pleated box, sporting pictures of band members. Lawrence thought that he might lease his idea and recipe to restaurants under contract and thus build up a nationwide business.

But first he bought a diner and began serving squeeze-burgers over the counter. The diner was at the juncture of two busy highways, U.S. 65 and 18, in Mason City, Iowa, a town through which he often traveled. He pro-ceeded to give his new property a face-lifting.

"The maestro loves gimmicks," says one of Lawrence's publicity men, who should know, as he has had something to do with a few of them, including the radios shaped like a champagne bottle with the cap of the bottle the dial; with the paint sets for children with pictures of Lawrence Welk in color; with the "Drive Carefully" windshield stickers "and enjoy Lawrence Welk's Champagne Music"; with the accordion-shaped earrings, and tie clasps; the pencils with tiny champagne bottle heads, and so on. Lawrence has these gadgets made up to give to his fans.

Naturally, then, he would set to work on his diner. He

revamped the outside of the place so that it looked like an accordion, and he redecorated the inside from top to bottom with novelties shaped like musical instruments.

Despite all his ingenuity, and grandiose plans of expansion, and despite the fact that diner profits were satisfactory, Lawrence did not stay in "the food business" long.

"When I went away, I left other people in charge," he says, "and they didn't pay much attention to business. Well, I couldn't take care of it myself, unless I neglected the band. There wasn't anything to do but sell it."

Where did he go when he went away? To no other place than California. In 1951, shortly after he acquired the diner, he was booked at the Claremont Hotel in Berkeley.

This particular journey to California was more important than he knew. It meant a shift of scene. Yes, Scene II of this Act III is laid in California.

♫

Chapter 28

"California, Here I Come"

"It all goes back to trying to do somebody a good turn. Mostly when we stop thinking of what we can get out of it, but are kind to folks because we should be, that's when we're most likely to have nice rewards come to us."

So Lawrence talks about what happened in Southern California in 1951, and the events which landed him with supersonic speed smack in front of TV cameras.

After he had finished up his job in the northern part of the state, he decided that, before he returned to home base in Chicago, he'd swing south through Texas and pick up a few jobs.

On the way he planned to stop in Los Angeles to make some recordings at Coral Studios. "There I was, real near the Aragon Ballroom," Lawrence says, "so I thought I should look up the manager, my old friend Pops Sadrup. I heard that he had his dander up high, because after I had played his place, I'd gone to a rival ballroom, the Palladium on Sunset Boulevard."

By taking the Palladium job Lawrence had not intended to sabotage the Aragon's business, and he planned to explain as much to Mr. Sadrup. "I never want to help myself by hurting the other fellow," he avows. "That's basically wrong, and in the long run, it's bad business, too."

When Pops Sadrup saw Lawrence, he began to talk shop. He grumbled to the maestro: "Fat chance I have of getting name bands for the price I can pay nowadays. The Aragon is losing money."

Lawrence listened and then made a spontaneous offer: "How would you like to sign us up? After all, we don't have to go to Texas."

"Are you kidding? The way things are, you know I won't be able to pay you the kind of dough you're used to. The union scale is all——"

"Tell you what I'll do," Lawrence cut in. "I'll come for four weeks on union scale, and a fifty-fifty split."

"It's a deal," Pops replied, "and I'll never forget you for it."

With that pet idea of his of going "one step further than is necessary to do the right thing," Lawrence was glad to make this conciliatory gesture.

He didn't know as he sealed the bargain with Sadrup that station KTLA-TV had been picking up the bands direct from the ballroom for a local program.

"I guess I wouldn't have been much impressed even if I'd known," he says. "We'd been on TV in New York two different nights, and we didn't set fire on the world."

For some time KTLA had featured whatever band happened to be at the Aragon. At the rate bands were usually changed, that meant a different band telecast every few weeks. The manager of the TV station, Klaus Landsberg, had used the program as a proving ground. If a band showed fan appeal on the Aragon tryout, anything could happen. A couple of times it had resulted in Landsberg finding the band a regular spot of its own at the station.

Prior to Lawrence Welk's appearance, however, being disappointed with the bands Sadrup had hired, Mr. Landsberg had discontinued telecasts from the Aragon, and the arrangement ended with Sadrup owing Landsberg money. "Get me Lawrence Welk," Landsberg had once prodded Pops, "and we'll work the thing out."

So Pops had Welk. There was only one possible hitch from Mr. Landsberg's viewpoint: Lawrence Welk's contract with Saderup to play his four-week Aragon engagement failed to mention telecasts. What if the Music Maker should object to that idea?

"I wasn't anxious to be on television," Lawrence admits. "I had all the confidence in the world in the band. But I didn't know how I'd be in front of a camera."

He was aware of his "country boy" personality. Before the implacable Cyclops eye of the camera, there would be no hiding the least quirk. Every detail, every gesture, would show up "big as life and twice as natural."

There wasn't much time to decide. The first telecast was arranged for the first week of his Aragon engagement. Despite fears and worries he must have considered the stakes large enough to warrant the gamble: his answer was yes.

The date was May 11, 1951. The show ran one hour, 10:30 to 11:30, and it had barely gone off the air when response from the public began trickling in to Channel 5. Phone calls, followed by letters the next day, commented favorably and often ended with the Oliver Twist request: "Please, sir, may I have some more?"

Before the month was out, and before Lawrence's contract with Sadrup was up, Lawrence had signed with the local KTLA station. The engagement was for four weeks.

So rang the opening gong for the Welk TV career!

His popularity didn't zoom rocketlike into the strato-sphere, but it did show healthy progress upward each week, as Lawrence tried "to do the right thing" morally as well as musically for his new TV audience, just as he al-ways had for his familiar ballroom and radio audience.

Even in those initial four weeks the show made some money for KTLA, which in itself speaks well for it. As the manager of any station knows, a new show is a gamble and even the eventually successful ones do not always prove lucrative from the start. Others make considerable money to begin with and then die quickly.

Under the circumstances could the contract be re-newed? If so, with the Aragon in the offing, Lawrence be-gan to wonder whether his hopes of anchoring on one of the coasts could become a reality.

Always an outdoor fellow, he liked California. He liked the climate which permitted him to sleep under the stars (without the blanket of snow such as nature provided in Denver the night Shirley was born) and the climate which allowed him to keep the top of his car down most of the year.

"I hadn't been there long when I decided to make the move, if I could," he says.

He had no sooner come to this decision, however, than he was ready to do an about-face and reverse it. He wasn't sure that he would, or in his opinion could, stay at the Aragon. He began to see that many patrons now came to the place, not to dance, but to use the hall as a hangout for cheap love-making sessions. Lawrence wanted none of that.

Promptly he went to the ballroom managers and told them so, asking them, at the same time, to police the place. Dumfounded, they demanded: "What do you think this is, a church?"

Lawrence didn't argue. He simply answered: "Do something about it or get yourself another band."

They quickly made promises, and Lawrence reinforced any efforts on the management's part with some of his own. There were instances when he left the bandstand to remonstrate with a petty would-be Lothario so positively that the man either changed his ways or else left the Aragon once and for all.

Watching the exhibition, the managers quaked in their boots. The Lawrence Welk band had been their bright hope to pull them out of the hole, and now what? Surely such tactics would only sink them deeper into the financial morass, for who would come to a Puritanical playground? Soon the place would be empty.

To their surprise nothing of the sort happened. Quite the contrary! The Aragon was attracting more customers every night, and of a different type than formerly, a type which gave the place a higher "tone."

Everybody was satisfied. As one man amazingly put it: "After all, you don't have to run a laundry to make money in a clean business."

Later even the small town of Ocean Park, usually described by Southern Californians as "a honky-tonk berg" began to spruce up a bit. Unwittingly Welk influence was fashioning a Pygmalion, a My Fair Lady.

Lawrence is still playing at the Aragon, which is the

all-time record for length of engagement of any name band at any ballroom in the United States.

He has added special features of his own devising. He has given teen-age matinee dances, during which the Aragon bar remains closed. "We should try to give decent entertainment," Lawrence says. "Not that entertainment alone will keep kids out of trouble if they haven't been taught the right thing at home and so don't want to be good. But if they want to be good in the first place, then decent entertainment may make it a little bit easier for them."

Also, to encourage graceful ballroom dancing rather than gymnastic cavorting, Lawrence holds his weekly dance contest for his usual patrons.

This is an amazingly beautiful pageant. The center of the floor is cleared, and then usually about thirty competing couples glide out over the polished surface, while the rest of the crowd stands in a wide ring, off in the shadows.

The very size of the place lends dignity, sweep, and perspective, as the couples whirl around till the full, beruffled gowns of the women flash every luscious color of an artist's fantasy. As somebody put it: "It's like a movie production of a palace ball. And the silent, intent spectators encircling the dancing couples are like courtiers, standing in the shadows."

Whatever Lawrence devises seems to take. The crowds seem to grow larger with the years. Police and fire guards are assigned to the building to make sure for the public's safety that the place does not bulge dangerously beyond its five thousand capacity.

But before all this happened, how did the local tele-

casts come along? And how about the move to the West
Coast?

After the first four-week contract with KTLA had run
its course, Landsberg had offered Lawrence a continued
weekly show. With this assurance, plus the Aragon, what
was Lawrence waiting for? The move to California was
only a matter of mechanical arrangements—or wasn't it?

Unexpectedly Lawrence found Fern reluctant to pull
up roots. She didn't want to give up the nearest thing she
had ever known to a permanent home, unless and until
it was as sure as taxes that California could offer as much.
Also she had a few misconceptions derived in part from
the tabloid press and the movies about Hollywood itself.
This made her wonder if it would be the best environment
for the children.

She says, "I was willing to wait a while and see. I didn't
want to rush right out and sell our River Forest house."

However, she adds: "Once Lawrence has made up his
mind—and especially about business matters—I don't, and
can't, hold out long with a different opinion."

In that she is like a great many other people. After
Lawrence once had Pete Fountain, the clarinet player
from New Orleans, on the show as guest, the bandleader
declared: "I want him for our band."

Several Welkmen repeated Lawrence's remark to Mr.
Fountain, but he shrugged it off with: "I'm proud to know
that Mr. Welk wants me, but I'm not interested in a new
job. I'm going to stay in New Orleans. I like the place."

This reaction was relayed to Lawrence and he said to
Larry, his son, and to Lois, his secretary: "I'll get Pete.
Wait and see."

"Dad, you can't do it," Larry protested. "I've talked to

him myself. He told me he'd never leave New Orleans."

Lois spoke up: "He told me the same thing."

"Wanna bet I can't get him?" challenged Lawrence.

"We know better than that," Lois answered for both of them. "Determination is your middle name."

Within a few days Lawrence had hired Pete Fountain.

Obviously Fern couldn't have held out long about moving to Southern California. But, to shorten the time that she might resist his sales talk, Lawrence began house hunting. He explains: "I figured that when Christmas came, since I couldn't get back East, she and the kids would be coming West for the holidays. Now, if I had a house all picked out and ready, Fern wouldn't keep putting me off."

Not a bad psychologist, our Lawrence!

He soon saw what he was looking for, too, and immediately made an offer through the real estate agent. However, since the offer was considerably below the asking price, it was refused.

Then Christmas did come and with it, "Fern and the kids." She saw the house of Lawrence's choice and liked it, but she didn't suggest that he raise his offer; as what woman wouldn't, she wanted to look further and see all the possibilities for herself before Lawrence had a deed to some house in his pocket.

The real estate agent was happy to show the Welks around, and he kept advocating larger and more pretentious places. They left Lawrence quite cold. Says he: "I thought a fancier house would be foolish, and even bad, like getting something just to live up with the Joneses. Anyway, I fell for the first place. Fern came to see that it was pretty nice too."

It was fine with both of them, then, when the agent called to tell Lawrence that his original bid had been accepted. Lawrence paid his money, and a house in Brentwood, a section of west Los Angeles, was his.

Meanwhile Fern had returned to Chicago. The plan was for her and the children to stay there until school closed in June. But everybody knows what happens to "the best laid schemes o' mice and men."

Long before June, Fern received an urgent SOS: come to California without delay!

Lawrence had practically collapsed on the bandstand.

♫

Chapter 29

"All or Nothing at All"

"I had a gall-bladder condition, which caused awful pain," Lawrence says. "One night it got impossible. I don't even know what happened. The pain was so bad that I was sort of foggy in my head, but somebody—I think one of the band members—led me off the bandstand and rushed me to the hospital."

As quickly as a plane would carry her, Fern arrived at her husband's side. She was there in time for the operation he had to undergo.

Recovery seemed rapid. Soon Lawrence was back at work, and urging Fern to return to Chicago to sell the River Forest house, and to make any other arrangements necessary for the move West at the close of the school year.

She had not been gone very long when, on another night, pain recurred to Lawrence, and with it came a weakness so extreme that he all but collapsed. Again he was led from the bandstand.

"The doctor said I shouldn't have gone back to work so quick," is his laconic explanation.

When Fern arrived in California in June, she was shocked to find her husband in an enfeebled state, existing on baby food and milk. She set to work to build him up. They lived in a motel with kitchen facilities, and she cooked him food that combined the qualities of digestibility, nourishment, and tastiness. In a few weeks Lawrence really recovered, and the family, with bright hopes for the future, moved into the Brentwood home.

As a year or so passed after that move, Fern was certainly convinced, if she had not been before, that the business setup for Lawrence in Hollywood was as permanent as anything of the kind could ever be. Especially was this so after Dodge sponsored the show.

But how did that come about?

As some people look at it, there might be a certain element of luck connected with it, but Lawrence himself says: "I just know that if we do our part as well as we can and leave results to the good Lord, then great things can happen—even great material things sometimes."

Before Dodge entered the picture, Champagne Music had been good enough to draw several sponsors, including Chicken of the Sea Tuna, and Laura Scudder Food Products.

Then Bert Carter, representative of Dodge dealers in Southern California, decided that he would like to see and hear Lawrence Welk in person, with the idea of considering the band as an advertisement medium. However, the Carter-Welk meeting hinged on a small incident.

To arrange the get-together, Jack Lavin (with Walt Disney) brought Mr. and Mrs. Carter and their subdeb daughter to the ballroom on a certain night, but because the young lady was underage, the doorman, according to the rules, refused them entrance.

If they had taken his word as final, and turned away before coming face to face with Lawrence, would the whole notion of the local Dodge-Welk combination have died a-borning? Lawrence was a comparative newcomer in Hollywood, and there is at least some doubt that Mr. Carter would have been persistent in seeking a chance to hear the band in person. Meanwhile there were other established entertainers he might have cast an eye toward instead.

As it happened, however, Jack Lavin managed to override objections, and escorted his friends into the ballroom to introduce them to Lawrence. The bandleader chatted amiably and apparently aimlessly. He didn't know that Bert Carter was looking him over for a purpose. But it wasn't long after that meeting that Lawrence had as sponsor the Dodge dealers of Southern California.

The next step—and it was a giant one—came when Jack Minor, an officer of the Dodge Company in Detroit, spotted the Welk show and exclaimed: "Why don't we have that band to advertise nationally?"

Shortly thereafter the company offered to sponsor the Lawrence Welk show for a summer replacement on a nationwide hookup.

"When they talked to me about it, I got a little dizzy," the bandleader confides. "I was crawling out on a limb if I signed up. It wasn't an easy decision to make."

He thought about it carefully and prayerfully. True, his "country boy" personality had gone over in Southern California, the Shangri-La of many retired Midwestern farm folk, but would it be equally acceptable throughout the United States? Since merely a summer replacement was offered, that question was crucial. If he did not go over very, very well—if indeed he were not a smash hit—

come fall, according to the usual fate of summer replacements, his show would be sidetracked to make room for the regulars. Moreover, if this fate awaited his band after he had left Landsberg for the nationwide job, would a spot remain open to him at the local KTLA?

"It was like the song 'All or Nothing at All,'" Lawrence points out.

But even so, he didn't delay overmuch in casting his vote for opportunity, reasoning: "If we look for security alone, that's all we'll ever have. We have to take some chances of loss, if we want the chance at big things."

The decision once arrived at, Lawrence turned eager-beaver, anxious to begin his new venture. However his contract with Landsberg had another year to run, so Lawrence told Dodge that he was not yet available for the national show.

"I could only hope they'd be willing to wait the year," Lawrence says.

That they did wait is, to the bandleader's mind, just one proof among many that he has "real wonderful bosses." He says further of them: "I couldn't work for finer people. At the time that they gave us a spot on national TV, there wouldn't have been another company in the country willing to take that chance. Nobody else believed that a dance band would go over so well on television."

With this big opportunity looming ahead the delay of one year was a terrible ordeal for Lawrence. He chafed under it, but he admits now: "It took me a long time to see, but that delay was really good for us. Knowing that the big show was coming up, I had a year to practice with it in mind. That helped. I got a lot of wrinkles ironed out during that time, and when the show did appear nationally, it had a better chance because of the extra work."

Those months of waiting were also useful in formulating policies. Many of Lawrence's associates held the opinion that, in order to make the show go over nationally, spectaculars should be added to it, as well as a line of shapely girls. To their surprise Lawrence, the neophyte in this TV medium, balked. He controverted the suggestions of the experts, saying that he wanted to present his show just as he had always had it. The flamboyance they urged might be all right, but . . . well, it wasn't his style. To him it seemed a little pagan.

"Now, Lawrence," they protested. "You're anxious to make the big time. OK, then, you have to have what it takes. Without a few chorus cuties, and a few acts, you won't last beyond summer. Out you'll go on your ear—and you'll be worse off than before you got into the thing."

Lawrence shook his head. His band, with one girl vocalist and no more, his band with no acts whatever, would take its chances. "Well, at least get a glamorous movie personality for an emcee," was another suggestion, vetoed by Lawrence.

"Guest artists! That's the answer," some bright-eyed idea man spoke up. "You need variety."

Lawrence considered. Since the day of America's Biggest Little Band, when six men played thirty-two instruments, in fact since the days of the Peerless Entertainers, when everybody did everybody else's job along with his own, variety was one thing Lawrence had striven for. He knew that he had variety within the band itself. Moreover he wanted the homey effect of having the same people week after week. "Folks will think of us as a family come to make a regular weekly visit. We don't need outsiders."

"How corny can you get?" The experts were aghast.

"I wouldn't mind making this a talent show," Lawrence countered. "I've always dreamed of some way to help gifted youngsters get a start. Maybe through the show . . ."

"Cut the kidding," came a regular chorus. "Dodge is taking a big enough chance on you and your band without loading the dice with unknown talent. What do you think this is?"

Two years later Dodge came to Lawrence proposing that he have a second show on Monday nights and try out his talent-quest notion. That second show, *Top Tunes and New Talent,* now rivals in popularity the first—that is, the Saturday-night show.

But in the days before the national hookup all this was very controversial. Also controversial was Lawrence's insistence upon only "good songs."

Naturally a song wasn't "good" if it was even slightly suggestive. Such a song called for Lawrence to protest in an aggrieved tone: "Fellows, you know we don't want anything like that on our show!"

At first some of the men argued back: "But you have to play all the popular numbers, regardless." Or they would say: "You should add zip to the show, or your rating won't rise."

"I don't want to win a public that way," Lawrence would answer. "Besides I don't even think that's the way to win the largest public. You hear a lot about the wrong kind of folks. They make headlines and scandals, so you think there are more of them than there really are. Anyway, let's please the good folks."

For a while his opponents continued such discussions: "If the majority are 'good folks' as you say, there are still plenty who can no more stomach entertainment without a dash of the sexy than an egg without salt. The way to keep everybody happy is to gear most of the show for your 'good folks,' but throw in a tidbit here and there to keep the other fellows tuned in too."

To that kind of reasoning Lawrence always responded by talking about the mother of a family. "Suppose she turns off the TV just once, because she thinks the kids shouldn't be listening to our show—well, the chances are that that family is through with us. They'll never again tune us in. What if we've gained a couple of loose fellows, if at the same time we've lost a whole family?"

Anybody who wanted to introduce an off-color lyric learned that he might as well forget the idea. Lawrence wouldn't listen. However, other differences of opinion continued to crop up occasionally. Lawrence would turn thumbs down on a lyric if he detected an idea at odds with any point in his basic philosophy, remarking: "Freedom of speech is a great blessing. We have to take care of it. The best way to take care of it is to say right and reasonable things, not things that ball up people's thinking. Then we prove that we can be trusted with freedom."

Sometimes his cohorts scarcely knew what he meant. For instance, a number of them were baffled when he made a little pronunciamento of this sort in vetoing the song which goes: "The good Lord is with you right or wrong." Lawrence had to explain: "Folks could take that different ways.

Lots of them might think it's telling them that God doesn't mind your doing wrong."

So it went. Obviously a great many policies were formulated by July 2, 1955, the date when Lawrence Welk first appeared on nationwide television.

Chapter 30

♪

"O Happy Day"

In the semiconsciousness of waking up the thought over-lay his mind: something big was to happen. Oh yes, this was the day! This was the day he was to go on national TV. Wonderful—and frightening!

"I went down to the studio with . . . what is it people say . . . butterflies flapping around in my stomach," Lawrence admits.

The show had been rehearsed thoroughly. Even so, he left his Brentwood home at 7:30 that morning for a last all-day session. Over and over the program went the twenty-two tense men, and one nervous girl, Alice Lon.

"Lawrence has always been a perfectionist," observes a long-time band member. "How do you think he got to the top in his profession if it isn't that one thing about him?"

Well, certainly on this day of days, the show had to be perfect. Not till five o'clock that afternoon did the band knock off, and then they had only one hour of relaxation before the show went on the air.

"I can relax anywhere," Lawrence will say. "On a tour, I can sleep bolt upright in a car. I can sleep on planes, in Pullman berths, on a day coach, even on floors." But he should add: "When I have nothing worrisome on my mind."

With the show on his mind that day Mr. Music Maker could not even sit down quietly. He paced back and forth across the stage, checking and rechecking to see that all was in order. He read over the "idiot" or cue cards, crayon scrawled with the announcements he would have to make. "I could hardly swallow," he says, describing his state. "I had a tight feeling around my neck like somebody was choking me and I kept remembering that there would be millions—really many millions of folks—listening every time I opened my mouth. I was afraid that I'd never get the words out."

He thought of those people. To him they were not a grayed mass. They were separate persons. He thought of Shirley and Bob, at that time living in Washington, D.C. He knew that Shirley would be listening, but would Bob be able to get away from his duties as intern in the hospital, at the very hour that he, Lawrence, would be on the air? He felt that Shirley would want to share with her young husband this experience of seeing her daddy cross-country.

He thought of Donna, who was visiting in Chicago. Nothing short of fire, flood, and earthquake combined would keep her away from the TV screen tonight. Affectionate, impulsive Donna! No doubt in her excitement she would practically go through the screen when she did see him.

He thought of Edna Stoner, the bedridden arthritic, in South Dakota, his loyal fan from the beginning. Would she be seeing him? Then his mind skipped to his sister Eva, working as a nurse in the very town where he had begun his career, Aberdeen, South Dakota. How about her? And his brother Mike, the only one of the family still living in the old house on the farm? Probably the show would not reach that area, even if Mike and his family owned a television set.

And there were George T. and Alma Kelly, now living in a small Wisconsin hamlet, would they have access to a TV set in a city which would carry the show? He wished he could thank all for the support and encouragement they had given him through the long struggle to these dizzy heights.

He glanced at his wrist watch. Was it running? Time seemed an incredible laggard as Lawrence waited for his zero hour. Nothing to do until then.

He looked out into the studio auditorium. Silence, like a fusty curtain, hung over the almost empty hall, and its thick folds engulfed his musicians, too, and himself. There was something preternatural about it.

Ah, there was Fern sitting calmly in the front row!

She rarely came to the Aragon, and she had never been one to drop in at any ballroom, radio station, hotel, or night club where he played. "And I don't encourage wives doing that. They don't really belong in a man's place of business," Lawrence will avow. But this was different! It was mighty good to have her at the Hollywood studio that night.

Self-consciously he grinned at her, and she smiled back placidly and reassuringly.

"A wonderful woman!" Lawrence murmured to himself, and a lump rose in his throat, as for some occult reason he remembered their hungry "honeymoon" in Chicago. Perhaps it was symbolic of all they had been through together.

Then he saw his son, Larry. A self-constituted private investigator, he was wandering about the studio, excitedly poking into this or that. Lawrence caught the boy's eye and received a reassuring grin.

Soon the guards posted at the doors admitted the crowd which had been outside waiting to see the show. Lawrence went backstage but he sneaked a look from the wings. He recognized faces here and there. Some were of folks who came weekly to the Aragon, some of friends of his in private life, some of course strangers.

As he studied the crowd, the guest director, Ralph Portner, appeared to make his little salutatory speech. Now it was Lawrence's turn.

So soon!

He struggled through the words he was supposed to say in his usual diffident fashion, and they were received with tremendous enthusiasm. He smiled at "the folks" gratefully, thinking: That was nice of them to give me a good hand.

Now there should only be about ten minutes more, the "warm-up time," as it is called in "show biz." He beckoned to Myron Floren. "How about a quick number?"

There was the entertainment to put the folks in a receptive mood for what was to come. Maybe he should also dance with a lady or two, if he could. He realized that he was sweating beneath his layer of pancake make-up, and that his hands were trembling.

He managed, flashing smile and all.

Then the music ended, and a silence more unearthly than ever descended. Its immensity was broken by one dramatic sound effect, the thump-thump of his own heart. But somehow he lived through the seeming eternity of it all, and at the precisely correct moment he heard himself utter his mystic formula: "Uh-one, and uh-two, and . . ." and music came in great bolstering swells.

From then on he was on "Champagne Time" skipping along at a quick, gay tempo.

But how did a show look to the viewers on television screens throughout the country? This thought hammered with muffled but steady beat in the back of Lawrence's mind, even while the fore part of his brain attended to the problems at hand.

He glanced up to see the sound man, there upon his perch, maneuvering his Martian-looking contraption. Then he followed with his eyes the cameraman, swooping and swiveling down to take close-ups. He even cast a quick look at the stagehands silently and expertly setting up props for the next number, as he was directing Alice Lon's solo.

The old three-ring circus had nothing on this!

Haphazard as all the activity might look to the studio audience, Lawrence knew that only the most rigid following of cues and time limits would allow the performance to proceed without mix-up.

"Talk about butterflies in your stomach. I guess by this time, I had eagles in mine," he says. "Only a few feet beyond the camera's range I'd see a stagehand run with a towel and dry ice to apply to the sweating jowls of one of the boys. I knew it was awful hot with those dozens and dozens of klieg lights, and I was used to them doing that same thing with the local show, but it scared me that night. I kept thinking, What if the camera should make a mistake and swing around and catch this?"

But as the classic poet puts it: "All's well that ends

well." Now people were swirling around, congratulating Lawrence.

Was it all real? He looked over the heads of the fans to his boys, the same fellows he had worked with day after day, and their faces seemed transfigured in light. Bob Lido's smile, for instance, seemed to make the boy's face into a veritable sun . . . and Barney Lidell was grinning . . . and Aladdin and Orie Amadeo . . . all of them.

Lawrence felt as though he had been transported to some strange new world—glorious, gorgeous, and quite ineffable.

Or was it just good familiar earth, heaped up with blessings. There at his side stood Lois, his secretary. Her smile, honest and wholesome as bread, met his boyish grin. He exclaimed: "Isn't TV wonderful!"

♫

Chapter 31

"Merrily We Roll Along"

Since the night of his nationwide première Lawrence Welk and his orchestra have appeared weekly on the TV screens of many millions of people, so that today only a Rip Van Winkle would ask: "Who's Lawrence Welk?" Everybody else knows.

And if the word "singer" is mentioned, someone is bound to bring Alice Lon, petticoats and all, into the conversation.

Indeed the individual boys of the band will never again be able to travel incognito, even so much as the length of one city block. Their faces are more familiar to the American public than those of the men who represent us on Capitol Hill.

Of course, since the first night, Lawrence has added a few new faces to the band—among them that of Larry Dean, "Tiny" Little, George Thow, Maurice Pearson, Jack Imel, Joe Feeney, and Pete Fountain. It has always been Lawrence Welk's policy to reinvest a good portion of his income to improve his organization. For example, five more members were recently added: Art Depew, Kenny Trimble, Jimmy Henderson, and Alvan Ashby. Most notable of all the additions, perhaps, are the very dear faces of the Lennon Sisters.

A sidelong glance at those little girls.

Their career began over the kitchen sink. Mrs. Lennon, the mother of nine children, naturally expected her daughters to help in the busy household, and she put the famous Lennon Sisters to work washing dishes. Throughout that nightly chore the girls would sing.

Papa Lennon (who, like his wife, looks only a few years older than Diane) was a former vaudeville singer and performer, so it was the most natural thing in the world for him to act as a sort of casual impresario to some of their sessions. On occasion he would help them harmonize with the aid of pitch pipe, and he would direct them by wielding a wooden-spoon baton.

But he didn't want his daughters to pursue show business in the way he had as a boy. He remembered the touring, the living in cheap hotels, the long, grueling hours, the lack of a stable home life.

"I wanted them to get in at the very top," he says.

Could there ever have been a more fantastic wish? The odds were $99^{94}/_{100}$ against it.

"But we did a lot of praying," Bill Lennon explains. "We have special devotion to St. Joseph, and we asked him to intercede for us that the girls would get the right kind of spot—at the top."

Meanwhile Bill plugged away at earning a living for his large brood without trying to augment the family income through the obvious talents of his children.

Then it happened that Diane, the eldest sister, who attended St. Monica's High School in Santa Monica, was invited by a classmate, Larry Welk, to a school dance.

It is doubtful that the thought even crossed her mind that the son of the famous bandleader was a good person to cultivate. At any rate, whether it did or not, she declined the date. She had promised to sing at a charity affair, the Catholic Women's Club Benefit.

Larry must have a little of his father's persistence. He said: "OK, I'll wait till after that's over, and we'll go to the dance late."

Larry hung around and listened while he was waiting. He had nothing else to do. "Gee whiz," he told Diane afterward, "I thought you were going to sing in a choir with a whole bunch of girls. I didn't think you had a swell sister act like that! It's terrific!"

Next day he repeated his high praise of the Lennon Sisters to his father, but Lawrence didn't appear interested, and "no," he couldn't "find time for an audition—not at all soon."

Aside to Fern the bandleader said: "All kids think their friends are wonderful. Larry doesn't have an ear for music."

Undoubtedly St. Joseph was on the job. A few weeks later Lawrence was in bed battling a heavy cold. It was then that young Larry maneuvered the Lennon Sisters into the house, and persuaded his father to give them a hearing.

What Lawrence heard amazed him. "Such perfectly blended voices! And real wonderful personalities, too!"

It was almost too good to be true. Was the penicillin he'd been taking giving him hallucinations? He had the girls audition for his producer, director, and musical supervisor. Opinion was unanimous: "The Lennon Sisters are a find of finds."

So from that day forward Diane, Peggy, Cathy, and Janet have appeared regularly on the Lawrence Welk show.

In the spring of 1957, Janet remarked before the Saturday-night cameras: "We have a new baby in our house. His name is going to be Joseph Lawrence."

She didn't explain the Joseph. Probably she thought explanation unnecessary. Anybody who knows the Lennon family knows that their devotion to St. Joseph would have prompted the name. But Janet did explain that the Lawrence is for young Larry, not Lawrence Senior. So the two patrons, the heavenly and the earthly, are honored.

However, if young Larry did a great deal for the Lennons, the Lennons, or the Lennon Sisters, have done a great deal for all the Welks. Those youngsters have done their bit and more to make the Lawrence Welk band wagon roll merrily along the highway of success.

But the personnel of the orchestra isn't everything. Equally as important to Lawrence's progress have been the policies he has followed. His insistence upon a simple, non-spectacular show and his rigid adherence to the wholesome have paid off.

Not that Lawrence devises his policies primarily to fill his pocketbook. In any aspect of his business moral considerations come first, then money. Says Sam Lutz: "I've seen Lawrence refuse fifty thousand dollars for an endorsement, just because he didn't particularly approve the product. But on the other hand, don't you ever try to gyp him out of so much as five dollars, or you'll be sorry. Lawrence hates injustice and he won't be taken."

Indeed the bandleader himself recounts: "Just before last Christmas some firm asked me to endorse their toy accordion. They wanted to put my picture in all the national magazines with a caption telling parents to get this accordion so their kids would learn to play. Well, I tried it out, and I saw it was a piece of junk that would fall apart in a week, so I turned the proposition down. Some of my associates thought I was foolish to pass up a few thousand dollars that I could get that easy."

The overriding motive behind any of Lawrence's policies (whether they are connected with the show or not) is unrelated to the monetary. Yet, in the words of a cohort of his: "These policies in the long run make money, or at least they have not prevented money-making. Lawrence rakes in the cash as fast as government mints can turn it out."

Didn't Chapter 1 mention that Lawrence Welk's 1956 income-tax report shows a gross of about three million? And as for 1957 it offered Uncle Sam even larger pickings. Then the other day somebody in the Welk organization made the flat prediction: "1958 is going to be the best year ever."

Along with the financial rewards have come the honors.

To rattle off a few that Lawrence has won within the last couple of years: in the fourteenth annual poll of *Radio Television Daily*, the nation's radio and television editors selected the Lawrence Welk show as The Musical Show of the Year; the National Ballroom Operators have dubbed the Lawrence Welk orchestra the No. 1 Dance Band of America; then Lawrence still holds the all-time record for a one-nighter attendance won back in 1954, when he drew a crowd of 51,233 at Blimp Hangar, Santa Ana Air Base; and he holds the record for the longest engagement at a ballroom by a name band, playing continuously at the Aragon Ballroom since 1951.

Heaped on top of these past honors come the new ones each day, so that by the time this is in print, there will be dozens more that could be listed. Indeed Lawrence cannot accept all that are offered him, because often the group or society making the award want to present him with a medal, plaque, scroll, or some such memento during his show. As his producers point out: "Much as he hates to do it, he has to turn them down, or even his fans would get sick of seeing him being handed something new on every show."

But one of the laurels he did accept, and proudly, was the honorary degree of Doctor of Fine Arts, conferred on him by University of Portland. "That wasn't something handed to me on the show. I was supposed to go to Oregon for that," he says. "On account of TV, though, I couldn't get away, so Fern went to accept it for me."

Another award he accepted gladly was that of Musical Father of the Year, and there he could be present to make an acceptance speech himself. His subject? To the astonishment of his confreres it was the Ten Commandments. "These laws given us by God," he declared, "should be stressed when we train our children."

But besides high-sounding honors, and record-breaking feats, Lawrence Welk has the recognition of vast numbers of John and Mary Does throughout the country. This goes far beyond that aforesaid business of being well known. In many cases it seems to go to the point of affection and real devotion.

Mr. Music Maker cannot go beyond his own front door without gathering well-wishers and autograph seekers with every step he takes. And they really mean it when they say: "I want to thank you for the happiness you've given me." Some of them also add: "I remember the night I first heard you in Sioux City . . . in Denver . . . in Dallas. I was dancing to your music when my husband proposed to me."

When Lawrence enters a restaurant or hotel, he draws a small crowd as quickly as though he blew a fire siren to announce his approach. While his party is ordering and eating, he will be signing menus, business cards, backs of envelopes, or any other blank surfaces that eager fans thrust under his nose. Only between signatures can he gulp a few bites and often he manages no more than a partial meal before it is time to leave for the next scheduled appointment. And says Fern: "That kind of thing seems to be building up all the time. Lawrence never buys gas without the folks in some passing car spotting him, and he never goes in a store, office, airport terminal, or club without being surrounded."

But perhaps a greater proof of progress than anything else is the demand for more Welk music. Because of that demand, in the fall of 1956, Lawrence uncorked another bottle of Champagne melodies and inaugurated his Monday-night show, *Top Tunes and New Talent*.

He was glad to do it, despite his already full-to-bursting life, because, he says: "It's always been a dream of mine to give talented kids a real break."

"Kids" of all ages, talented and otherwise, are eager to make the show. Tape recordings by the hundreds pour into the Santa Monica office. Lawrence now has a talent committee who handle the auditions under his direction. Also, he has arranged with Daughter Shirley to act as his Eastern talent scout. At the rate things are going there is not the slightest danger that he will run out of talent before the year 2010.

So the two full hours of nationwide television time with approximately two hundred stations carrying his shows are his indefinitely. Besides that his record sales run a million a year, and dance dates and radio contracts are his to the extent that he can squeeze them into his tight schedule.

No doubt about it, Lawrence Welk and the boys roll along merrily with Champagne Music still fizzing away.

♫

Chapter 32

"Dear Hearts and Gentle People"

So much for the events of Lawrence Welk's life. The tale is told. It seems to fall neatly and naturally into separate acts, like a play. But I, the writer who put the story on paper, also indulged in a little prologue to present the man and to pose the problem to be solved.

Now there must be an epilogue. I need it because I haven't quite made good my boast. I boasted that I could uncover the clues and, in the end, expose the mystery, the how-done-it of Lawrence's success. There are still some elusive bits to bring out.

Nor have I revealed in full the who-is-he-really of the man. I contracted to do that, too. I must fit in some mighty important segments before all the other pieces of the jig-saw puzzle make sense and the whole man springs into full view.

I know what's missing.

The night before I was to leave the Welk home, I glanced over my notes. I had the outline for the story as I have presented it here, and I was satisfied that it was reasonably complete. Then I began packing. As I was collecting a pile of papers, magazines, and so on, a portfolio slipped out and fell to the floor. From it spilled a letter and a picture.

They struck me as symbols. In a flash they brought to my mind the question I had asked Lawrence almost in the very beginning: "Who helped you most toward success?" and his answer: "The folks who liked our music" and "Fern and the kids."

I picked up my souvenirs—or symbols. Had I sufficiently emphasized the two, and had I even looked at them from *every* angle? After all, it was true, Lawrence's fans and family did further his success; also they help reveal the man.

I opened the letter and spread it out. It was given to me by one of the boys, and it was written by Lawrence to the band members and intended only for their eyes. I reread it, and here are a few sentences from it: "Going to a dance is an occasion for most folks. The housewife usually has her hair done, and then she dresses up in her party dress, and the husband changes from his work clothes to his carefully pressed best suit. That evening the couple go to the dance, and stand around watching, dressed up and excited, but a little bashful. That's why you've heard me say: 'Hi, folks. Nice to have you with us. What tune would you like?' It breaks the ice. You boys can do a lot to make folks feel at home too."

Now, doesn't that help round out what I've written so far? Lawrence thinks of the people he plays for today just as though they were the folks who came to barn dances back in the Dakotas, and he thinks of himself, not only as a bandleader, but also as a host at a party, enjoying himself with his neighbors.

"Lawrence Welk has never lost touch with the public," is a much-repeated Hollywood remark, but it doesn't say all. Lawrence Welk is not in touch with a public outside himself; he is *of* it, *of* the folks. He knows what they like, mainly because it is what he likes himself.

That picture? I picked it up and studied it. It was the usual family group, showing Mother, Father, and children —the Welks. I think, to round out the man completely, I'll have to end up with an extra bit in this epilogue just about the Welk home and my stay in it.

But first I want to finish with the fans.

When I asked a newcomer to the band about his boss, he spoke surprisingly about a picnic that Lawrence gave for the fans. It occurred a couple of weeks before my California arrival. I'm sorry I missed it, but here's this musician's description.

"The affair wasn't publicized. Just by word of mouth of his fan club of Southern California,* three thousand people showed up—and were fed at Lawrence's expense.

"I arrived with my wife and kid, and looked around for him. He wasn't in sight, but I told my wife, who was dying to meet him: 'Oh, he'll probably drop by for a few handshakes, and then leave. Going through this crowd would be like going through a wringer. You can't expect him to take it for long.'

"I had hardly finished speaking when I spied Lawrence. Dressed up in a chef's hat and apron, he was standing at the head of a long table, dishing out food. Four hours later, he was still going strong.

"But that wasn't all. After lunch he played with the kids —different kinds of games, including baseball, with the

---

* There are eighteen Lawrence Welk fan clubs. Mary Lee Schaefer of Los Angeles is president of the national fan club.

little-leaguers he sponsors.* He ended up by giving out prizes to the winners of the competitive games and dancing with the gals. One gal, a two-year-old tot, kept begging: 'Dance me.' He had 'em all ages."

Then did he succumb to battle fatigue? Not Lawrence!

According to the teller of the tale, the picnic ended at 6 P.M. to allow Lawrence to get to the Aragon at the usual time, where it was play and play on till the wee hours.

Anything for the fans!

And Lawrence finds endless ways of reaching his fans. He sends out a booklet, "magazet," as he calls it, entitled *Sweet Notes of Friendship*. He doesn't write or edit it himself, but he does pass on its contents of light verse, prose quotations, and short articles, which, as he says, plug "the good way of life."

Then Lawrence has always taken his fan mail with tremendous seriousness. Up till 1950 he read every letter himself, and he would find time in a car, or plane, to dictate personal answers. Today, with thousands of letters weekly, that kind of thing is almost impossible, but he does keep a private line of communication open to many chosen souls. Among them is Edna Stoner, and she is one reason why this epilogue is being written. I think that I gained much greater perspective on the Lawrence Welk career, as well as glimpsed more side lights on the Lawrence Welk portrait, by stepping back and looking at them through the eyes of this girl, whose own life story is entwined with that of the Music Maker.

After I returned to my East Coast home from the California sojourn, I corresponded with her and with other

---

* They appeared on the Lawrence Welk show in May 1957.

long-standing Welk fans, and here's Edna's story as I pieced it together.

In 1927 she was a pretty youngster with laughing Irish eyes of clearest blue—and a love of dancing. She lived in Beresford, South Dakota. When the Lawrence Welk band played in the area, Edna and her high-school crowd would get up a party to go to the local ballroom. Later after Lawrence began his first regular radio program at WNAX, Yankton, she and a boy in the neighborhood would often whirl about to the gay music in her own living room.

But in the fall of 1928 something happened to Edna. She would wake in the night with pain in all her joints. The doctor diagnosed arthritis, and in December, just after Christmas, Edna was sent to a Sioux Falls hospital for "rest and treatment."

Still the disease hurried on, twisting her hands and feet into odd, contorted shapes. On January 13, 1929—Edna has no trouble remembering the exact date—the doctor broke the news: she would be bedridden the rest of her life.

For the fifteen-year-old girl with laughing eyes that was a blow which doubled her up in mental anguish as surely as the disease doubled her up in physical pain. She could see only loneliness and isolation ahead. How face it?

"Aside from my faith and my grand family," she says, "my biggest help was my radio friends. Like a little girl, I made believe they were real friends, who came to visit me through my loud-speaker. Lawrence Welk was my favorite. I always listened to his program. I had to play games with myself, so I began trying to find out about my friend Lawrence's life and career. It was fun when I discovered a new fact."

When Lawrence left Yankton for a few years, Edna heard him only occasionally until the spring of 1934 brought him back to WNAX. "The band stayed two and a half years this time, and I'm sure I didn't miss one broadcast," she avows. "And did I chew a lot of Honolulu Fruit Gum!"

When Lawrence was to play in the evening at some nearby town, he would announce it on his morning radio program, and if Edna was not familiar with the place, part of her "game" was to look it up on her road map and make believe she was there. "I did extensive imaginary traveling that way," she avers.

In the fall of 1936, Lawrence left for Omaha (and subsequently went on to other far places), so thereafter Edna could rarely tune in the band.

But one bleak night in January 1938, after a gray, dreary day, Edna's sister happened to twirl the dial of the bedside radio, and over the sound waves came gay, sparkling rhythm. Unmistakably that was Lawrence Welk's orchestra. The music emanated from the William Penn in Pittsburgh, and soon the announcer referred to Champagne Music.

"That name! It's perfect!" Edna exclaimed, and then, impulsively turning to her sister, she requested: "How about writing Lawrence Welk for me?"

Until then she had never written him. "It didn't even cross my mind that he would be interested in knowing how much I enjoyed his music," she explains, and "besides," she adds, "my—well, my hands."

Edna's hands were too badly crippled to guide pen or pencil. But now she wanted so much to congratulate Lawrence on the name, and on his success, that she was impelled to ask her sister's help, adding excitedly: "I kept telling everybody that someday he'd outstrip Guy Lombardo, Wayne King, or Jan Garber, all of them. Now that he's at the William Penn, I know he's all set to go."

This young arthritic, and virtual recluse, had more vision than Lawrence's agents and bookers. Back in 1938 she saw clearly the heights ahead.

And ever since 1938, Lawrence and Edna have been corresponding. In answer to her first letter he sent her a short note, along with his picture, and a schedule of his broadcasts.

After that, as she continued to write him, he sent her postal cards of places where he was playing, as well as newspaper write-ups, pictures, and trinkets.

But it was the very first slim packet of material which suggested a way to enlarge her game. Edna decided to start a Lawrence Welk scrapbook. Today she says: "I have six books filled with cards, letters, pictures, clippings, and souvenirs, and I have enough stuff to fill several more books. My sisters and I are working on them now."

In the fall of 1944 the band was on tour in South Dakota, and Lawrence darted off his beaten track to visit Edna in Beresford. He took his Champagne Lady, Jayne Walton, and a couple of the boys with him, and right there in Edna's bedroom they gave an impromptu concert, playing all her favorite tunes. In parting they dubbed her No. 1 Fan.

Since the first visit Lawrence and a few of the boys show up at Edna's whenever a South Dakota tour brings them near Beresford. Then in 1948 the maestro, being booked to play at the Corn Palace in Mitchell, South Dakota, sent an ambulance the 107 miles to Beresford to pick up Edna and her two sisters and bring them to the afternoon show. After the show he invited them to join him and some of the boys for a dinner party backstage.

What a thrill for Edna!

But since then there have been many thrills Edna speaks of: "Trips to Tom Archer's ballroom, the Arkota in Sioux Falls, a tape recording of interviews between Lawrence and myself, and, best of all, I guess, what happened in July 1949. That was when I, as Lawrence's No. 1 Fan, was his guest on his coast-to-coast radio program for Miller High-Life beer."

After the broadcast Edna received letters from all over the country. By this time she had learned to write with her twisted hands, so she answered them herself—and lo, she had pen pals.

Magazine articles about her followed, and in turn more pen pals. Today she can truthfully say: "I'm not lonely any more. I have many friends even if I don't see them. Lawrence Welk fans and fellow sufferers of arthritis, too, write me all the time. I love corresponding with them, and all of this came through Lawrence. He'll never know the happiness he's brought me."

One pen pal in Winner, South Dakota, belonged, as it happened, to both the arthritic and Welk fan category, so she and Edna decided to meet at the Corn Palace four years ago, when Lawrence played there again, and again sent an ambulance the 107 miles for Edna. This time he gave a big dinner party for her in a private room of the local hotel. She described the evening by saying: "I felt just like Cinderella, escorted to the ball by Prince Charming. I was so happy it never occurred to me that it must have looked strange to other people to see me being carried and wheeled into the ballroom on an ambulance cot."

Lawrence's kindness to Edna is not a mere fan-pleasing maneuver. He is sincerely devoted to her. When I met him in Washington on Inauguration Day, one of the first things he said to me was: "I got word that Edna Stoner's father died."

On the day of his great triumph he thought of her and her grief.

Of course all of Lawrence's fans are not so charming as this arthritic girl. He draws a few "characters." Watching him handle them gave me another slant on the Lawrence Welk portrait.

One night when I was sitting in the Welk living room with all the family (except Lawrence, who had gone to a recording session) a shadow seemed to glide past the picture window.

"A ghost," young Larry said matter-of-factly, and then, taking pity on my mystification, he explained: "Dad's women fans sometimes have the weird habit of walking up and down in front of the house trying to get a glimpse of him. We call 'em ghosts."

He went on to tell me about the ghosts who write gushy letters, and he produced one fit for a psychiatrist's pondering. In it a woman told Lawrence that she had read in the stars that he was her soul mate. And shortly after the haunting-of-the-house episode some woman wrote to him saying: "If you play my favorite song at the Aragon tonight, I'll take it as a sign that you'll meet me at closing time."

Lawrence made a mental note of the song, not in order to play it, but to be sure that he would avoid it. However, as luck would have it, when he stepped from the bandstand a minute, the strains of that very song assailed his ears.

As he left the ballroom later, this particular ghost took on flesh and rushed toward him, exclaiming: "At last!"

"Lady," protested Lawrence sternly, breaking the hold she had on his arm, "I'm a family man."

With that he was in his car and away.

But there are others like her—and worse. "It isn't always funny," Fern said. "The original ghost, as the children called her, was a poor demented woman in Chicago. She threatened to jump from the Trianon balcony if Lawrence didn't pay attention to her. Then she threatened to kidnap the children. We had to notify the police."

And then, of course, there are the ubiquitous F.F.F.s. To even the most desirable and persistent of them Lawrence always manages to give what he calls, the "fluff-off."

"With the letter writers, it's easy," he says, though he admits: "Yes, there are an awful lot of them," and "Yes, they do have love on the brain."

They often ask his age and marital status. One woman explained that she was particularly interested in this data because she was a widow, and she added: "For your information, my home is worth $10,000."

The gush, the goo, the giggles do not affect him. He repeats: "The folks we want to please are sensible, honest people—homebodies."

Occasionally he will receive an angry note berating him for failure to grant a request. One of these letters, picked at random, has to do with a discount on a car, and it reads: "Do you think I would have written you in the first place if I could get a discount from my local dealer? You must be dumb to refer me to him."

"Some fan mail you can't take seriously," Lawrence says. "That kind of faultfinding isn't sensible. Lots of praise isn't sensible either; it's exaggerated. I pay attention to suggestions and requests for songs, and I really appreciate it a lot when folks write nice friendly letters."

Among the "nice" letters was one from a mother telling about her four-year-old. At the end of the program, just after Larry Hooper's deep bass had come in with: "Dodge had a good time too," the child remarked solemnly: "Mommie, God's always having a good time on the Lawrence Welk show, isn't He?"

Besides letters gifts also deluge the Welks. "We get stormed under sometimes," Lawrence puts it. Anything from a sack of potatoes, sent by a farmer, to a pipe organ may appear upon their doorstep, or at the office, or TV studio.

One day the local express man phoned and told Fern: "Two pheasants and two peacocks have arrived for you, air express. They are addressed to the office. What do you want me to do with them?"

Fern, thinking in terms of pheasant hunting back in North Dakota, and of the many birds she had canned for food, answered: "Just go ahead and deliver them. Mr. Welk can have them put in the deep freeze."

"I don't think you understand," came the reply. "These are *live* birds."

Every gift seems to add to Lawrence's sense of gratitude to the "wonderful folks." One way he tries to repay them is by the many thousands of dollars' worth of trinkets he gives out to his fans. The night I met him, and we went on to the Aragon, I was loaded down with a small assortment of pens, pencils, records, key rings, etc.

But his gratitude is best shown by his thoughtful concern for his fans. What happened in Houston, Texas, is a good example. He was to play there, and a week before his arrival every ticket for the three-thousand-capacity auditorium was given out gratis—courtesy of Dodge. But scalpers somehow obtained a cache of the free tickets which they proceeded to sell at ten dollars each. When Lawrence reached the auditorium the night of the show, he heard about this "funny business." Instead of being flattered that people had been willing to pay a premium to hear him, he "blew off the handle," and insisted that the auditorium manager find out who, among the crowd, had paid for admittance.

Some people who had obtained tickets irregularly were at first reluctant to give their names and addresses. As one man explained: "I didn't know what was up, a penalty, maybe. At best, I thought we might be asked to leave."

Nothing of the sort.

The next week those who had given the information received by mail a check signed "Lawrence Welk," to cover the ticket price.

Of course he also favors his fans with benefit performances when he can. Unless, or until, another day is added to the weekly calendar, he could not be more generous in squeezing charity affairs into his bursting schedule. At the same time he says: "I don't like to use my religious donations for publicity."

"And that's as it should be," says one of his fans.

But why do I keep calling them fans? I mean friends, don't I?

Chapter 33

♫

"Home, Sweet Home"

Now, with the photograph before me, I'll get to the missing piece of the jigsaw puzzle and the final clue to the mystery story, Lawrence's family and home life.

I shall never forget the first time I entered the Maison Welk. It was that Saturday afternoon when, en route to the studio, I stopped by the place with Ed Spaulding. Of course I had only a quick preview, yet it was downright startling in its revelation.

I stepped from the California sunshine, still bright and shimmering despite the later afternoon hour, into a cool, shaded interior, and immediately I seemed to be enveloped by an almost tangible serenity. I glanced around, perhaps to notice vaguely the soft gray-green walls and carpeting that contributed to this effect, but I didn't take them in, not really. I had glimpsed, and then instantly my eyes had been pulled toward one object.

Looking the length of the living room, and on through the master bedroom beyond, I saw, exactly framed in a far window opening on the garden, a large statue of the Virgin. The arms were outstretched in a simple gesture, as though to embrace all children of mortal man, and especially, so it struck me, those who enter this house. There was a soft

luminosity and an ethereal quality emanating from the
thing, partly due, so Donna told me, to a bluish bulb hidden in the dark cluster of shrubbery. It cast a faint glow
on the white figure, and made the leafy growth around it
play with delicate light and shadow on its stone surface. I
could only exclaim: "How lovely!"

Is it significant? Does it mean that Lawrence Welk and
his family live within the aura and influence of a simple
religious faith? That was the question I asked myself. After
I had stayed with them awhile, I could answer only one
way.

Sunday is the big family day. It begins when all the
Welks go to Mass together, and then gather in the small
breakfast nook off the kitchen for a leisurely brunch, at
which Lawrence himself sometimes turns chef.

The first Sunday I was there, the morning after my arrival, I was rather surprised when Lawrence asked: "Like
me to fix you some scrambled eggs?"

During the day he often plays a game of ping-pong with
Donna or Larry, and almost always he puts in a long-
distance phone call to Shirley and Bob.

At 2 P.M. Lois arrives with a list of songs requiring Lawrence's selection for the next Saturday's show, but this
doesn't take long, so he can rejoin his family at an early
afternoon dinner. Throughout the week he wedges in odd
intervals with his family and he declares: "I really do enjoy those breaks. I used to play golf, ride horseback, or
hunt, but nowadays when I have so little free time, I hate
to use it for anything but my family."

In 1956 Lawrence and Fern celebrated their twenty-fifth
wedding anniversary with a party. "Fern is the original
ministering angel!" claimed one of the guests.

True, she spends her life ministering to the needs of husband and children. She strictly regulates Lawrence's diet, limited by a digestive ailment.

Having heard of this, I was taken aback when I heard him ask Fern one night, as he was about to leave for the Aragon: "Where's my bottle? Did you slip it in the car for me?"

The "bottle" turned out to be a thermos jug, filled with skim milk. Were, or are, the patrons ever disconcerted if they see him take a nip from it? Or would they surmise the truth: that he was seeking nourishment and stimulation from nothing stronger than milk?

Their conjectures don't bother Fern. She is thinking about Lawrence, and she feels that he requires sustenance through the long hours till 3 A.M.

Habitually his health is one of her prime concerns. When he must eat a whole meal on the fly, she packs him a lunch box. Three guesses what's in it. Often canned baby food. Fern knows that this bland concoction is guaranteed not to upset his temperamental insides, especially when food must be gulped in seconds flat. It should also facilitate, I would imagine, Lawrence's weight control. "I try to keep around 177 pounds, and no more," he told me.

Home meals are not set by the clock but by Lawrence's engagements. On Friday the dinner hour is advanced to 5 P.M., because, says Fern: "I like to have it early enough to give Lawrence a chance to take a nap before his long session at the Aragon."

And she is there to wake him gently lest he oversleep, that is, if the impetuous and affectionate Donna hasn't beat her to it, by rushing in the bedroom and kissing him back to consciousness. (Any excuse is enough for her to give her dad a bear hug and a few quick kisses.) Then, if he is pressed for time, the whole family may crowd around to hand him socks, cuff links, tie, etc., though Lawrence points out: "Usually that's not necessary. Usually I arrange things so that I don't have to hurry, because the ballroom is a fair distance. It's a rosary away."

Meaning? Why, that he has time to say the rosary beads through between home and the Aragon.

Who but Lawrence would so measure distance? But then many things about the Welks are "different." Their life is a strange enclave in the Hollywood hullabaloo. I was really struck by this when I looked at Lawrence and Fern acting out their parental role.

I remember the day I asked Lawrence: "What ambitions do you have for the children?"

He answered: "We want them to be good."

That stark reply left me momentarily speechless, and I was still fumbling for words to ask: "But would you like one of them to pursue a musical career?" when Fern spoke up: "Whatever job or profession they choose, we just hope they'll remember what we're trying to teach them now—definite standards of right and wrong."

I could see how she and Lawrence went about it. I arrived in California shortly after young Larry, then sixteen, had become involved in a little misadventure. With his driver's license a fairly new acquisition, he had gone out on a certain afternoon in his father's black and white Dodge convertible. He was traveling along the highway, just a few miles an hour above the speed limit, but no faster than the cars on either side or in back of him. There was no passing at the time. Then he heard the traffic cop's siren, and the next thing he knew he was being ordered to pull to the side of the road. A few minutes later he held a traffic summons.

The poor kid was crushed, and he was scared. How could he tell his father? A couple of days later he screwed up courage and blurted out the story. For a moment Lawrence said nothing, then he asked: "You *were* over the speed limit?"

"But only a few miles over, honest, Pop. And everybody else on the highway was going along at the same clip. I think the cop spotted me, 'cause I'm a teen-ager. Bet he thought I didn't have a license."

"I'm sorry," said Lawrence. "I know how awful bad you must feel. But after all you did do wrong. You broke the law. That's what counts. Of course lots of people try to use that excuse of yours: 'Everybody's doing it,' but it's not a real excuse. We shouldn't let other folks decide for us. And we can do right no matter how tough it is. God helps those who help themselves."

"But what about the summons?" Larry asked woefully. "What if they revoke my license?"

"Oh, Daddy, do something," wailed Donna, all sympathy for her brother.

If she meant: Please, Daddy, use "pull," Lawrence didn't understand the plea. He just laid a comforting hand on her shoulder, and murmured: "Now, Donna."

The next day Larry went down to the traffic court to take whatever medicine was measured out for him. Happily, the magistrate did not revoke the license; he simply forbade the boy to use a car on dates or on personal business for one month. Since Larry had a summer job as band boy, he was permitted to drive on errands for his father.

While I was staying with the Welks, Lawrence gave him

properly official instructions to drive me on all my book-connected expeditions. The boy's wisecracks and jokes enlivened every trip. I didn't repay him very well, for I kept him waiting many a time, as I interviewed some Hollywooder about Mr. Music Maker. Larry's patience and politeness were evidence enough of excellent parental training.

And that training certainly tells a great deal about Lawrence and his alter ego, the girl he married.

"With Lawrence away so much, I had to be both Mother and Father," Fern explained to me. "Only of late years has he been home regularly, but we certainly couldn't wait that long to begin training our children. In fact, I believe that you have to start training a child in the crib. If you pick up a baby every single time he whimpers, he will get the idea that his own wishes are all that matter, and ever after he'll make 'I wanna' his guiding star."

Fern's definite notions which she stated so matter-of-factly were backed up by Lawrence. He sat there nodding agreement as she spoke.

"You can love a baby just as much while you're teaching him that there are rules to follow," she said, adding after a moment's reflection, "Maybe you love him more because you make it easier for him later when he is on his own."

"Fern's own life is lived right," Lawrence remarked. "Our kids have her to go by."

"I've found that kids take your regulations in stride if you put over while they're little that what you ask them to do isn't just a crazy whim; it's the right thing, it's what we're all trying to live up to."

"And we love our kids an awful lot," added Lawrence.

"They knew we wouldn't ask them to do something which wasn't real good for them."

"With plenty of love, we didn't have to use stiff punishments. Good thing, too!" Fern smiled toward her husband. "Lawrence couldn't have stood them. I guess you've heard about the time when Donna and Larry were little . . ."

It seems that Donna and Larry were squabbling. Lawrence's repeated "Be quiet" did not stop them. He told each child to hold out a hand on which he duly administered a slap. Instantly he was greeted with howls of distress.

He began to wonder if he had hit harder than he intended. Screams and sobs continued and each reverberated painfully in Lawrence's nervous system. Finally, about to break down himself, he put his arms around the children and drew them toward him. "I'm real sorry I had to punish you," he said. "Do you think it might make you feel better if I gave you each fifty cents?"

He produced the coins, and tears and howls ceased like magic.

The next morning Fern was in the kitchen preparing breakfast when little Larry came in and told her about the incident, commenting: "You know, Mom, we like *Daddy* to punish us." Then, lest his mother miss the full implication of his words, he added: "It's worth fifty cents."

Perhaps I should append the footnote: there are no more spats between Donna and Larry today, and none with Shirley, either.

Shirley, however, will admit that there were times years ago when a younger sister and brother proved a nuisance.

She tells about one of her first dates: "This boy was calling to take me to a prom, and Donna, who was peering through the window, saw him coming, so she rushed to open the front door, and yelled over her shoulder: 'Gee, Mom, he's just as good-looking as Shirley said he was.' Talk about being embarrassed! I couldn't look him straight in the face all evening."

But today Shirley says about Donna: "Isn't she refreshing? She's so spontaneous!"

And about Larry she says: "A generous kid if I ever saw one, and such a lot of fun."

Then the two younger children say about Shirley: "She's tops. Mom thinks she's the one that's most like Daddy."

For Lawrence a single word, "wonderful," fits all his offspring.

"He's a sentimentalist about the kids," Fern declared, though she quickly admitted: "He can be firm when he really should. We both want our children to accept responsibility for what they do. From the time they were little we've tried to train them so that when they grow up they can stand on their own two feet."

When Shirley was leaving home for Marquette University, she asked: "Any last-minute instructions, Mother?"

"None whatever," Fern answered. "Your father and I have taught you what's right for seventeen years. Now it's time for you to prove that you've learned something."

"Of course you've taught her 'what's right' and, as Lawrence says, 'the law of God,' but let me ask next: How do you apply that law to money and strictly material things?" I turned to Fern with the question.

"We've tried to use the heads God gave us, and buy the kids what's best for them, not just anything in sight," she replied. "For instance, one time Shirley saw a formal she wanted in a shop in Milwaukee's Schroeder Hotel. It was seventy-five dollars. I thought that was too much for a young girl to pay for a dress, though we could afford it. I told her: 'Find something else you like for less money.' Some parents don't seem to think of what's good for the child; they think about themselves, and they have the idea that they can buy their children's affection with extravagance. I ask you: does that make sense?"

"All I know is that they certainly love you, Fern," I answered. Then to Lawrence I added: "Maybe you don't rate too badly either. When I first met Donna I asked her to give me a word picture of her dad. I remember how her face lit up, and she exclaimed: 'Oh, isn't he terrific? And he's so much fun, too. He's always pulling jokes. We never know what he'll think of next.' Not many young sophisticates talk like that."

"Donna's a great kid," Lawrence beamed. "Did I tell you about her horse?"

"Before you tell that story, let me explain that Donna simply dotes on horses," Fern put in. "She always has. When she was a little girl, I remember her saying to me: 'Mommie, when I grow up, do I have to have babies?' I answered: 'Well, darling, I hope you will have babies. Don't you want them?' She came back with: 'Babies are OK, but I'd rather have horses.'"

Lawrence chuckled: "Yes, Donna sure loves horses! And she can ride well. You've seen that trophy in the recreation room. She's won it at a horse show. A few years ago she begged me to buy her a horse of her own. I wouldn't say straight yes or no. But she didn't keep asking. I guess she figured that if I thought it was good for her to have, she would get it.

"I was busy, so I put off doing anything about it. Fact is, I almost forgot all about it, and a lot of time went by—

a couple of years, maybe. Then one afternoon I was home with a few hours free, and I remembered the horse. I picked up the phone and called a lady who had a mare for sale.

"She came right over to the house, and we sat down in the living room to talk business. I could see Donna through the doorway into the next room. She was walking up and down, wringing her hands, and moving her lips like she was praying.

"When I gave the lady a check for the horse and she left, I went in to tell Donna the news. And do you know what? She threw herself into my arms and burst into tears. She cried harder than I have ever seen her cry in my whole life. She said to me: 'Oh, Daddy, I think I would have died if you hadn't bought it.'

"That was the way she felt, but she never pestered me to buy that horse for her."

"Yes, despite her natural impulsiveness, she can use self-discipline," Fern commented.

"I've heard about that self-discipline," I said. "Sam Lutz tells of taking your children to a ball game some years ago, when they were tiny, and having them decline ice-cream cones, because they thought he shouldn't be spending money on them. But," I added, "that shows that you've also taught your children the value of money, which reminds me to ask: Do you consider wealth an obstacle in bringing up children to be godly people?"

Lawrence answered thoughtfully: "Almost anything we have we can use for either good or bad. Maybe it's harder for a rich man not to be selfish than it is for a poor man not to be envious . . . I don't know. But I do know that goodness has nothing to do with how much or how little

we have. It's the way we think about it, how much we let
it mean to us. We shouldn't let it come ahead of more important things."

As he spoke I recalled some comments of Shirley's. She
had said: "Mother and Daddy are so unworldly. Of course
Daddy never thought of himself as lacking so-called advantages or being comparatively poor as a boy; and he
doesn't often think of his high tax bracket now. He taught
us not to waste, but at the same time he never bothered to
explain much about money matters to us. While I was at
school, I had a joint checking account with Mother. I was
supposed to pay all my expenses, including board and tui-
tion. Once in a while, I'd overdraw the account, and I'd
get a little note from Mother, chiding me gently: 'Now,
dear, you must be more careful,' but neither she nor I ever
knew what the balance was. And when my canceled checks
came, I didn't know what to make of them. Bob has been
laughing ever since the day I told him that I used to wonder why the bank sent me those old things. I figured that
they didn't have enough scrap baskets."

But Lawrence does realize to an extent that handling
money is power and responsibility, and he is definite, as
Shirley says, about waste. "We don't want our children to
grow up thinking: Easy it comes, easy it goes," he declares.

Apparently they have learned that lesson. When
Donna finished at St. Monica High a few years ago, Lawrence told her that she could take a trip East as a gradua-
tion gift. She went by coach, explaining: "I'm young, and
maybe it would be foolish to pay extra for a Pullman."

Though when I heard it I called that the story of the
year, there is one to match. Lawrence mentioned: "I told
Donna I'd pay her a salary this summer to handle some

fan mail, and to help around the house.* Donna did her
job real fine, but when I got ready to give her the first
pay check, she said: 'No, Daddy, I shouldn't take it. You're
paying my way through college.'"

That story almost broke up our session for the day! I
nearly fell over backwards like a comic-strip character.
However, I managed to compose myself in time to ask
a couple more questions: "You pay Larry a salary for being band boy, and running errands?"

"Oh yes," Lawrence answered, "but he puts half of it by
for his college education. He can't touch that part."

"What happens if he runs short of spending money? Or
has that ever happened?" I pumped.

"It happened," Fern admitted. "Just the other day he
asked for a five-dollar loan, and I told him: 'If you borrow
now when things are easy for you, you'll probably borrow
later in life when maybe things won't be so easy. This may
be a good lesson. It may save you lots of future headaches
and heartaches, if you learn to buy only what you can pay
for.'"

"Folks have to learn self-control and independence, even
if they do have money," Lawrence commented.

I am sure that the Welk children have learned it. When
Shirley married Bob (then an intern on a slim salary) in
September 1954, she and he furnished their home only with
necessities. Of course, these did not include a TV set. However, when Lawrence was scheduled to appear on the network the following July, Shirley did want a TV "to see
Daddy's show." Now all she would have had to do was say

---

* The Welks keep no regular maid. Incredible as it may seem, they
employ domestically only a gardener, and a weekly cleaning woman.
Fern, truly a homebody, prefers taking care of the house herself.

so loudly enough and a dozen TV manufacturers, seeing the publicity value of the gesture, would have vied with one another in delivering the desideratum. Instead she kept mum and bought her own set, a secondhand one she could afford.

"But it's not only about money that our kids are independent," Lawrence assured me. "They're independent all the way down the line," and he added: "To be independent—independent of men, that is—you have to depend on God. My kids know that when they have God behind them, then they can have faith in themselves."

Have they acquired that attitude from their father? And has that attitude had an effect on the Lawrence Welk success story?

Chapter 34

♫

"I'm Forever Blowing Bubbles"

It was a Sunday morning, and I was about to say "*Auf Wiedersehen*" to the Welks and leave California for home and the East Coast.

As I closed my suitcase, I was running over in my mind the words I had originally scribbled down in my notebook as a beginning for this book: "Unbelievable is the word for him. Lawrence Welk is a wonder in gaudy and giddy Hollywood."

No change. I still held that opinion. Talk about your Puritan in Babylon, or your Connecticut Yankee in King Arthur's Court, if you will, Lawrence Welk is no less an anomaly in show business. Yet his special Welk way has paid off. Even though he disregards many sacred canons of the business, he has vaulted to the top of the heap. "How has he done it? What has he got? What makes the man tick?"

Those were the questions I started with. Well, I figured by that Sunday morning I had the answers. Now, it is about time for me to set them down on paper.

It should not be so very difficult to find words to answer the first question about his means to success. His life has been unraveled, and the clues brought to light and built up into a body of evidence. His hard work, his boundless energy, his drive, his enterprising spirit, his persistence, his concentration, his singleness of purpose, his sincere love of people and his earnest desire to please them, his musical talent, and his enthusiasm for music, which makes his job a joy—all of these are factors. Also, there is his sharp eye to see and his strong hand to grasp the name of every passing opportunity; there is his willingness to go, as he says, "one step further than is necessary, or that I'm paid for"; there's his business acumen coupled with a flare for showmanship; there's his patient striving to make every tiny detail precisely perfect. There's his keenness to sense popular reaction which amounts almost to identification with "the folks"; there's his Geiger-counter ability to spot talent and his patience and skill in developing it; there's his power to inspire loyalty and—yes, love—among the "boys" with whom he so gladly shares the spotlight.

Add it all up and does it equal success with a capital *S?* Not quite necessarily and inevitably. How about the overriding intangible of personality? The mystery of Lawrence Welk's career triumph cannot be fully explained till there is a solution to the puzzle of the man himself, and answers found to the questions "What's he got?" and "What makes the guy tick?"

These are tricky questions, since Lawrence Welk is a somewhat contradictory son of Adam. On one hand, he is a canny businessman, with the calculating powers of a statistician and the caution of a banker; on the other he is a naïve romanticist, ever ready to ride off on a quixotic quest. He is deliberate, slow-moving as a tortoise—sometimes; at others impulsive, precipitous, a man who gladly takes a leap in the dark. Ordinarily he possesses a limitless

patience, but look out for the once-in-a-while; when a fuse
is lit by some unexpected circumstance, he can flare up
with amazing suddenness. And although Lawrence is self-
conscious about his speech and accent, the minute he
begins to play or to direct, he is the most completely self-
forgetting and most other-fellow-conscious person imagi-
nable. From then on he is concerned only about what he
can do to give happiness to everybody else; never, never
does he think about what kind of an impression *he* is making in order to gratify his own ego. Certainly he is shy,
but it is also true that he has a species of assurance and
confidence that no power on earth can shake. Finally, I
might add that, although Lawrence Welk is as predictable
as sunrise in many of his reactions, I understand what
Shirley means when she says: "I think I know my own father, but I still find him full of surprises."

I was sifting these ideas on that last morning, and formulating my final answer to the Lawrence Welk puzzle,
when he spoke to me: "Before you leave," he said, picking
up my bags and moving toward the front door, "are there
any last-minute questions?"

So, with my coat and hat on, ready to step over the
threshold, I put to Mr. Music Maker himself the questions
I was turning over in my mind: "How would you sum up
your own character? And what is there about you as a
man, as an individual person, which makes for success?"

He turned so that his eyes met mine, and then deliberately he set down my suitcases. We stood facing one another a long minute, before he spoke.

"Back on the farm, we kids learned what makes for real
success," he began. "You know, people talk a lot nowadays
about giving kids advantages, and usually they're talking

about things money can buy. We had better kind of advantages, and more security, too. We were taught that there was an Almighty God, we could look to for strength, when the going was tough. That's worth more than anything. It's with you even if the bank fails, the crop's ruined, and you're hungry for a meal that's not in sight.

"Then we had lots of love in our family among ourselves, and we believed in a loving God, too, Who would listen to our troubles. We were never alone, like the poor folks who don't have any faith.

"You know, years ago I found out that this music business I am in can have some very hard and hectic conditions. One time when I was in the dithers with a thousand details somebody real wise told me: 'Young man, don't try to do it alone.' He meant I should ask God's help. If I have any secret, that's it. Religion isn't just going to church on Sundays. It's something you have to try to live every day of the week, every minute of the day. Lots of times, when a whole crowd of people rush up to me for autographs and pull at my clothes, and hem me in so I feel like I can't breathe, I want to run away and hide. But then I look to God, and I offer my uncomfortable condition up to Him, as a thank-you prayer for all He's done for me. Whenever the going is specially tough, that's the only thing that helps me through.

"And turning to God makes me strong in lots of other ways. In our business, we don't have much chance to go off and think quietly, but the more fussed and confused I am, the more I need to keep a little quiet spot inside me, where I can talk to God, and think about religion.

"When religion shows me that a thing is right, that makes it easier for me to stand up against different kinds of pressure. Besides that, prayer and trying to look at ourselves as God must see us keeps a person on a better level. It stops us from getting too puffed out with pride. And of course, it helps too because it makes us work on ourselves to grow better. If I don't work on myself, I find that I go backwards.

"As a kid, and even later, I had a bad temper. It showed that time I used my whip on the lazy plow horse, and that way broke my arm. That temper could have been the ruin of my career. When things didn't go smooth, I used to scowl something awful, but folks in an audience don't come to see frowns. Without religion to show me that I should have better self-control I would probably never be able to hold my temper in. Trying to smile just to please customers doesn't work every time. What works is religion, teaching us that God wants us to do the right thing and be nice and kind always.

"Then I'd say that religion helped me take bad disappointments. I've had plenty of them along the way. Because I could trust in God, I could go on anyhow, knowing that if I did my very best, I'd get success provided I was meant to have it; but if I wasn't meant to have it, I'd be given the grace to take the awful bad trial of failure. That kind of thinking which comes in prayer kept me from going off deep ends, lots of times."

As he finished speaking, I could only murmur: "Thanks, Lawrence. You've thrown a great deal of light on the riddle of yourself."

And so he had! In fact I'd say that he had turned a veritable floodlight on the Lawrence Welk puzzle.

Before he gave his little dissertation, I was considering naming, as my prime hint to the solution, the quality of simplicity and unworldliness. After he spoke, I heavily underlined those two words in my notebook.

Now, by simplicity I do not mean that Lawrence, with his contradictory traits and personality quirks, is devoid of complexity. I do mean that Lawrence Welk is a creature who walks amid a world, peopled by its own admission with many a phony, yet he himself seems to be encased in a kind of armor of innocence and wholesomeness, and deep spiritual faith.

Amid the glitter, the glory, the guff, and the gags surrounding him he remains plain Lawrence Welk, sans make-up against the bombastic stage set of the twentieth century.

Indeed he *is* almost unbelievable! He is a strange creature, impervious to the very atmosphere itself. Its amorality does not affect Lawrence Welk as it affects—or infects —most of us, glazing us over with a monotonous, brittle shell of quasi-sophistication.

He holds to his original ideas. They go back to his boyhood on the farm, back to the roots of life. They are not overlaid or confused by superficialities, which parade as the last word or the latest wrinkle.

Moreover, he belongs to that rarest of all human species: he is the creature who does not put up a front, who does not play-act, who does not resort to sham or pretense, who does not take the expedient way, varying chameleon-wise to fit the occasion. Without contrivance he is what he is. Result: a genuine 14-karat man—natural, unique, or, I repeat, a simple, unworldly person, possessing the wonderful, untarnished, childlike wisdom which believes in truth, in love, in decency, in toil, in individual effort, in home, and in country.

Some people condescendingly include his kind of wisdom when they use the epithet "corny." Call it anything you like. When the personality of the man of that wisdom was presented over the air waves, the public welcomed it like a fresh breeze from the tilled fields. They loved it.

Surprising how much they did love it—or is it?

Maybe there is something under the pancake make-up of all of us which wants to believe too, which wants to accept ancient and ageless values, and maybe that something accounts in the final analysis for Lawrence Welk's fabulous success career-wise. Positively—and no maybe about it—his own simple, unworldly belief in ageless values, and his endeavor to live by them, accounts for his success as a man.

In the flicker of show business popularity can disappear overnight, making Lawrence Welk, the TV idol, a Hollywood has-been, but Lawrence Welk will remain a success as a man for one reason. Bill Lennon puts it into these words: "Lawrence lives with God."

There, "Ladies and Gemamin," you have it: the key to the puzzle, the master clue to Mr. Music Maker, Lawrence Welk.

Larry Hooper
Tiny Little, Jr.
Myron Floren
Jerry Burke
Buddy Merrill
Buddy Hayes
Johnny Klein
Jack Imel
Aladdin
Bob Lido
Dick Kesner
Billy Wright
Alice Lon
Jim Roberts
Maurice Pearson
Joe Feeney
The Lennon Sisters: Diane, Peggy, Kathy, and Janet
Orie Amodeo
Russ Klein
Jack Martin
Bill Page
Dick Dale
Pete Fountain
Norman Bailey
Art Depew
George Thow
Rocky Rockwell
Jimmy Henderson
Barney Liddell
Kenny Trimble
Pete Lofthouse
Alvan Ashby
Larry Dean
Curt Ramsey